Front Office Management

FRONT OFFICE MANAGEMENT

DR. Raj Kumar Singh
D.H.C.T. Mgmt. (W.B.)
P.G.D.B. Mgmt. (U.P.)
C.F.N. (Delhi)
MHCIMA (London)
Ph.D. (Management)
Director
'SAMS' Institute of Hotel Management,
Varanasi

AMAN PUBLICATIONS
NEW DELHI (INDIA)

Published by
Rajiv Jain for Aman Publications
LG-4A, Ganpati Bhawan,
4675-B/21, Ansari Road,
Darya Ganj, Delhi - 110002
PH: 23255012, 23282127
E-mail: sshjbs@yahoo.com

First Edition 2006
Reprinted-2010

ISBN-81-8204-012-4 (HB)

SOLE DISTRIBUTOR
JINDAL BOOK SERVICES
LG-4A, Ganpati Bhawan,
4675-B/21, Ansari Road,
Darya Ganj, Delhi - 110002

Laser Typesetting by:
S.M. Graphics, Delhi,

Printed by:
NCT Printers & Publishers , Delhi, India

PREFACE

The front office department of a hotel is the control centre for the organisation. Communication and accounting are two of the most important functions of a front desk operation. Effective communication with guests, employees and other departments of the hotel are paramount in projecting a hospitable image. Accounting procedures, involving charges to registered and non-registered hotel accounts are also important in the hospitality field. The front desk also provides strategic directions to the organisation for setting priorities, establishing policies, approving appraisal plans and schedules, administering the organisation, and developing and maintaining the necessary infrastructure. The sole priority of the front office department is to ensure guest satisfaction, which happens when, guest expectations match what the hotel provides.

This comprehensive book provides all essential information on front office management. It uses a human resources approach to cover the unique management and operational challenges in the front offices of today's hotels and lodging facilities. While its emphasis is on applying theory and management strategies, it also provides new material on technology's role in the modernised front office. It will be an invaluable book for those interested in learning more about the hotel's front office.

CONTENTS

1

FRONT OFFICE OPERATIONS

Hotels are amongst the most visible and important aspects of a country's infrastructure. Hotel industry is a closely linked one to the tourism industry. A number of factors like promotion of tourism and rapid industrial progress have given a boost to hoteliering. The recent liberalisation of trade and opening up of economy will further lead to revolutionary growth in this sector.

With increasing globalisation, career opportunities in this field are not only limited within the country but there are chains of hotels which operate internationally providing scope of a career abroad. It is a glamorous profession which has a bright future. With the growth of hotel industry propelled by foreign and domestic tourism and business travel, the demand for well trained quality personnel too has grown impressively.

The diversity of experience in hotel management is greater than in any other profession. Hotel industry involves combination of various skills like management, food and beverage service, housekeeping, front office operation, sales and marketing, accounting. Today, the rise in corporate activity (leading to greater number of business trips) as well as the wish to travel on holiday has made the hotel industry a very competitive one.

Guest Cycle

The guest cycle describes the activities that each guest passes by from the moment he/she calls to communicate a reservation inquiry till he/she departs from the hotel. Each stage of the guest cycle is associated guest service, and guest accounting activities.

— *Guest services*:
  — Reservation
  — Registration
  — Occupancy services
  — Check-out and history
— *Guest Accounting*:
  — Establishment of credits
  — Posting charges
  — Night auditing
  — settlement of accounts

In fact, the guest cycle encompasses 4 different stages, which are depicted in the underneath diagram:
— Pre-Arrival
— Arrival
— Occupancy
— Departure

Pre-arrival

At the pre-arrival stage, the hotel must create for every potential guest a reservation Record. Doing this initiates the hotel guest cycle. Moreover, reservation records help personalise guest services and appropriately schedule needed staff and facilities

The reservation department should, then, complete all the pre-registration activities and prepare guest folios (applicable only for automated systems). Doing so will eventually maximise room sales by accurately monitoring room availability and forecasting room revenues

Arrival

At the arrival stage, registration and rooming functions takes place and the hotel establishes a business relationship with the guest.

The check-in clerk should determine the guest's reservation status (i.e. pre-registered guests versus walk-ins). Later, he/she shall prepare a registration record or make the guest sign the already-printed pre-registration record (under some of the semi-automated and all fully automated systems). The registration records shall include the following personal and financial items:

- *Personal information*:
  - Name and Surname of the guest along with billing address, telephone number, and any other coordinates
  - Passport number, birth certificate, and/or driving license number (whatever applicable)
  - Any special needs or requests
  - Guest Signature
- *Financial information*:
  - Date of arrival
  - Expected date of departure or length of stay depending on how the system in the hotel is designed
  - Assigned room number

— Assigned room rate

— Guest's intended method of payment

Registration records can be used for various purposes:

— Satisfy guest needs

— Forecast room occupancies

— Settle properly guest accounts

— Establish guest history records at check-out [personal & financial information]

— Assign a room type and a room rate for each guest

— Determine long-run availability [i.e. reservation information] versus short-run availability [i.e. room status]

— Satisfy special categories of guests such as disabled people through barrier-free designs

Occupancy

At the occupancy stage, the front office department shall coordinate guest services in a timely and accurate manner. Moreover, front office clerks should encourage repeat guests by paying a great attention to guest complaints. This is ensured by placing complaint and/or suggestion cards in every public place and revenue centers in the hotel. Moreover, the hotel shall, at least on a daily basis, collect comment cards, proceed with their analysis, and provide positive feedback to guest as soon as possible. In addition, shall design effective procedures in order to protect the funds and valuables of guests. This might be ensured through guest key control, property surveillance, safe deposit boxes, and well designed emergency panels and exits.

Another activity at occupancy is to process posting of guest charges [i.e. post room rates, F&B charges, additional expenses, and taxes.] to various guest folios, master Folios. While doing so, front office clerks shall continuously check for deviations from the house limit, and take corrective measures as to change the status of the guest to Paid-in-advance. Finally, front office clerks shall periodically review Account Balances in coordination with the night auditor.

Departure

At the departure stage, the guest shall be walked out of the hotel. Moreover, front office clerks shall create guest history record. Finally, cashiers shall settle guest account outstanding balances [i.e.: balance the Guest account to 0] In general, a proper checkout occurs when the guest:

— Vacates the room

— Receives an accurate settlement of the guest account

— Returns room keys

— Leaves the hotel

At departure, checkout personnel should encourage guests to consider returning to the hotel on any future date. That's why cashiers should act like a true sales person, and might eventually accept guest future reservations. That way, the stages of the guest cycle become really a cycle (i.e. start from where it ends). If at departure, the guest account is not fully settled, then late charges accumulates. In such an undesired case, the responsibility of collection lies within the accounting department, however the front office department shall provide all necessary types of information to make this collection easier, quicker, and feasible.

Front Office Systems

Until the 1960's, nearly all hotels were operating under the manual system. At late 70's, with the introduction of computers, hotels shifted to semi-automated systems. Nowadays, most of the five-star hotels operate under the fully automated system. Below is a brief description of the three different systems under which hotels might operate.

— *Non-automated [manual] systems*: This very system is the one characterised by the sole usage of hands. In fact, all formats, procedures, and different kinds of calculations are done manually.

— *Semi-automated [Electro-mechanical] systems*: This system gets use of some Electro-mechanical equipment. In fact, under the semi-automated system, each department might have its own computer system under which it handles all its operations.

— *Fully automated [computer based] systems*: That's the best system ever used in the hotel industry. In fact, it is characterised by the excessive use of departmental software package programs integrated and connected to a main frame or terminal situated at the front office department.

Guest Cycle under Three Different Systems: Following stages of the guest cycle under the three different systems do not conflict with each other. In fact, the only differences are due to the nature of the system use. Therefore, what will be discussed above is not the repetition of the sequence; rather only differences will be highlighted.

Non-automated Systems

Pre-arrival activities: At the pre-arrival stage, reservation requests should be introduced in a loose-leaf notebook or index card. Moreover, only reservations up to 6 months horizons shall be honoured. Lastly, it is not practical, under this very system, to issue reservation confirmation numbers, initiate pre-registration activities (at the exception of VIP and groups) and prepare occupancy forecasts. The reason is, time and money loss along with insufficient labour force to manually conduct all the above mentioned activities.

Arrival activities: At the arrival stage, guests shall either sign a page in the registration book or fill manually a registration record. Under this very system, the most widely used front office equipment is the room rack, in which registration records are inserted to serve as room rack slips. Moreover, registration books and records shall be time stamped as an internal control proving when the guest exactly came, who registered him/her. Lastly, guest folios shall be opened for each registered guest.

Occupancy activities: Under the occupancy activities, registration records shall be prepared with multi-copies. In fact, one copy shall be distributed to room rack, another stamped to the guest folio, another given to switchboard operators, and a final copy handed to the uniformed service personnel. Lastly, guests with charge privileges charges and payments shall be posted to respective guest folios.

Departure activities: At departure stage, cashiers should settle each guest account's outstanding balance and get room keys back from guests. Moreover, cashiers shall notify the housekeeping department that the room is no more occupied (i.e. room status change) to let this very department clean the room and prepare it for new arrivals. In addition, cashiers shall remove room rack slips from room racks to indicate departure. Lastly, these very rack slips of departed guests shall be filed in a cardboard box to serve as a guest history record

Semi-automated Systems

This very system is less common in small and middle size hotels. For, these very hotels, financially wise, might not afford the huge investments associated with the installation of different hardware and software. The main advantage of this very system over manual system is that various reports can automatically be generated. However, the major disadvantages associated with this system are various complexities of operating and controlling devices due to the fact that these equipment are not integrated with other systems and are subject to frequent maintenance problems.

Pre-arrival activities: At this very stage, guests can either call a national reservation network or directly contact the hotel. Moreover, reservation clerks can prepare pre-registration records, guest folios, and information rack slips.

Arrival activities: At this very stage, already reserved guests shall verify their pre-registration forms and have only to sign it. On the other hand, walk-ins shall complete a multiple copy registration record from the beginning.

Occupancy activities: At the occupancy stage, in order to track the different guest charge expenditures and all other possible guest transactions, hotels get an intensive use of various kinds of vouchers. Moreover, the most widely used equipment, under this very stage, is the mechanical cash registers and front office posting machines. Lastly, under this very stage, night auditor shall continuously resolve any discrepancy in guest accounts and efficiently reconcile guest folios.

Departure activities: At this very stage, cashiers shall relay room status information to the housekeeping department. Moreover, they should place registration records of departed guests in property's guest history files.

Fully Automated Systems

Pre-arrival activities: Under this stage, the reservation department is equipped with a software package, which is interfaced and connected with one or more central reservation office(s). Moreover, the reservation department can automatically generate letters of confirmation, produce requests for guest deposits and handle pre-registration activities for all types of guests and generate daily expected arrival lists, occupancy and revenue forecast list.

Arrival activities: At this stage, various reservation records can be transferred to front office department. Moreover, hotels might be equipped with an on-line credit authorisation terminals for timely Credit Card Approval, self check-in/check-out terminals. Lastly, all guest charges and payments are saved in electronic guest folios. As far as walk-ins are concerned, all registration activities should be initiated from the very beginning.

Occupancy activities: Under this very stage, guest purchases at different revenue outlets are electronically transferred and posted to appropriate guest accounts. Moreover, the front office department can run and process continuous trial balances and, therefore, eliminate the tedious work for the Night Auditor.

Departure activities: At this very stage, cashiers can automatically produce bills to be sent to various guests with direct billing privileges and create electronic guest history records.

FRONT OFFICE FORMS

At different stages of the guest cycle different forms are used depending on which operating system a hotel chooses. Below are some of the common forms used:

— Pre-arrival activities:

  — Reservation record or a reservation file

  — Letter of confirmation

  — Reservation rack and reservation rack slips

- Arrival activities:
  - Registration card (or record) or registration file
  - Room rack and room rack slips
- Occupancy activities:
  - *Guest folio*: shall be of duplicate forms and pre-numbered for cross-indexing control purposes
  - *Vouchers*: support documents detailing facts of a transaction, but does not replace the source document (i.e. the invoice). Examples of vouchers might include charge vouchers, allowance vouchers, paid-out voucher, and correction vouchers.
  - Information rack slips
- Departure activities:
  - Credit card vouchers
  - Cash vouchers
  - Personal check vouchers
  - Transfer vouchers
  - Guest history records

Front Office Functional Organisation

Whatsoever system and setting the hotel might use, it should reflect easy access to the equipment, forms, and supplies necessary. Moreover, the setting shall reflect position flexibility. Moreover, nowadays trend shows that traditional mail, message, and key racks are unnecessary at the Front Desk. Rather, they shall be stored in drawers or slots located under or away from the Front Desk. For, this would ensure security and safety of guests.

Front Desk designed alternatives:

- *Circular or semi-circular structure*: this very structure provides an effective service to more guests and appears more modern and innovative but since guests will approach the Front Desk from all angles, more staff is needed.

— *Traditional straight desk*: Under this very design, fewer staff is needed, but fewer guests can be served at the same time.

— *Deskless environment*: Under this design, there is no Front Desk at all. This is usually replaced by a hostess, or steward welcoming the guest, seating him or her on a chair/sofa, and conduct registration activities there while, for example, having a cocktail or a drink.

Front Office Equipment

Front office equipments are:

— Room rack
— Mail, message, and key racks
— Reservation racks
— Information racks
— Folio trays or folio buckets
— Account posting machine
— Voucher racks
— Cash registers
— Telephone equipment

2

FRONT OFFICE RESPONSIBILITIES

The work of a receptionist involves spending a lot of time dealing with guest enquiries of all descriptions. The ability to answer guest enquiries accurately and promptly is the key to good customer service. While it may not be possible to know all the answers, to all questions, all the time, there are steps you can take to ensure that each guest enquiry is dealt with satisfactorily.

TYPES OF ENQUIRY

The type of enquiry you can expect to get on reception usually falls into three categories:

— *Reservation*: to deal with enquiries about reservations either over the telephone or in person, the receptionist must have on hand up-to-the-minute information of room status, the advance reservation chart, and the hotel directory and room rates/tariffs.

— *Information for the guest*: guests have come to expect reception staff to have all sorts of information at their fingertips. Enquiries can range from the cost of sending a postcard to Europe, to car rental facilities, to information on places of interest in the locality.

— *Information regarding guests:* enquiries about guests should be handled with caution and discretion. All guests are entitled to a measure of privacy and protection and any person requesting information about a guest, for example, the name and room number of a resident, should be referred to a supervisor or manager.

Receptionists are right if they believe that the customer expects them to know everything. Of course you cannot know everything, but it should be in your power to satisfy the guest's need, whatever the nature of the enquiry. As this is the service that is most likely to be in demand from reception or the information desk, you should build up your knowledge, particularly of the most frequently asked questions. These may include information on:

- the hotel facilities and services
- the locality—geographic location
- the locality—places of interest
- local services, e.g. transport, places of worship, airline offices, etc.
- entertainment—restaurants, theatre, etc
- additionally, foreign visitors may request information on local customs, cultural issues and language.

So while it may not be possible for the receptionist to have the answers to all questions, it is important to know where to get the answer and how. Every effort should be made to assist the guest with his enquiry. To do so promptly and accurately will require you having access to a range of information directories. You should have:

- a list of all the facilities and services in the hotel, with details such as opening times
- a list of names of members of staff, their job titles and telephone extensions

— details of what is happening from day-to-day throughout the hotel

— a good idea of what goes on in the locality so that you can inform guests looking for details of church services, entertainment and so on

— good reference sources to hand, such as local papers (for entertainment, shopping), telephone and trade directories, relevant street maps and so on

— timetables of local transport services

— tourist guide book of the region

Having the information on hand is of no use unless you know how to use the reference material you have. Make sure you find out how to use the reference books in the hotel to get the information you need—know how to use the index system, read timetables and interpret the postal tariffs. Adopt a simple general procedure to deal with standard enquiries:

— Greet the customer with a smile.

— Listen carefully to find out the requirements.

— Make a note of the relevant details if necessary.

— To avoid misunderstandings, repeat the main points back to the customer. Take special care if the enquiry is complicated, or the person has difficulty hearing.

— Ask further questions if you still are unclear.

— Deal with the enquiry immediately.

If the enquiry is for information

— Offer the options: "There are a lot of restaurants available around here, Sir. "Describe some of the options available.

— Recommend a course of action, for example, ".May I suggest you try our Italian restaurant on the ground level?"

— Offer to do the legwork "I'll just check for you Sir."
— Confirm what has been arranged, if applicable: "That's a table for four at 8 p.m. this evening."
— Finish the exchange on a positive now: "I hope you enjoy your meal."

If the enquiry is for service

Many requests or enquiries are received which do not involve information, the guest wishes to have, for example, extra towels. Requests for assistance of this kind could be received by telephone or in person. The basic principles of dealing with a general enquiry remain the same with the inclusion of two important steps:

— Record or log the requests in the reception log box. Note the room number, request details, time request were received, action taken, e.g. reported to housekeeping, your initials. If any follow-up action is taken this should be recorded in a similar way.
— Notify the appropriate department, e.g. housekeeping if the request is for extra towels, maintenance if the air-conditioner is not working and so on.

You should always try and deal with a guest enquiry yourself as it is very annoying for the guest if he has to ask several different staff members the same question. However there will be times when you cannot answer the enquiry and will have to direct the guest elsewhere. You should know what type of enquiries it is better not to try to answer but to pass on to the appropriate person. Some examples of these may include:

— What special discounts can be given to a group booking—refer to the front office manager or another senior manager
— Whether the hotel can accommodate a wedding on a particular day- refer to the banqueting manager

— Can the receptionist book an airline seat—refer to the local travel agent

The important points to remember when referring enquiries elsewhere are:

— Know who it should be referred to

— Explain to the guest why be you are referring it

— Do so promptly

LEADING WITH EMERGENCY

You should be aware of enquiry situations, which could be regarded as emergencies, requiring an immediate and urgent response, for example, and a request for medical attention. Each hotel will have its own procedure for dealing with these situations and you should familiarise yourself with the practice in your hotel. Very often the principle will remain the same:

— Ascertain the facts

— Repeat and confirm the essential details

— Action immediately—it is usual in emergency situations to contact the supervisor or manager immediately

— Record the incident in the reception log book

In cases of emergency the essential points to remember are:

— *Remain calm and act immediately*: Remember that the most important part of the enquiry process is communication. Effective communication—with guest, colleagues and interdepartmental is essential to ensure a high level of customer service and guest satisfaction.

Keep this checklist with you as a useful reminder of what you should do not should not do when dealing with guest enquiries.

— Do:
  — Be helpful
  — Have up-to-date information on hand
  — Know where and how to find the answer
  — Respond promptly
  — Record the details (if appropriate)
  — Take Immediate action
  — Notify other departments as needed
  — Follow up if necessary
— Don't:
  — Say you don't know
  — Forget to do what you set out to do
  — Delay

MAIL AND MESSAGE HANDLING

When handling mail and messages it is important to process them promptly and efficiently. This is good customer relations practice where the principles of speed, accuracy and professionalism are all key to "getting the job done" to the highest possible standard. The range of mail and messages you are likely to be dealing with are:

— *Incoming mail*: Received via the postal system, mail may arrive for various departments in the hotel, hotel guests and staff. With the arrival of new technology it is now possible to receive "letters" by Facsimile (the fax machine) or via the computer terminal, which is known as electronic mail or e-mail.
— *Outgoing mail*: Letters and packages for posting.
— *Messages*: Telephone and personal messages for your own and other departments in the hotel and hotel guests.

Mail Handling Procedure

It is necessary to have a procedure for receiving, recording and distributing all types of incoming mail both for guests and the hotel to ensure that the right message gets to the right person with the minimum delay. A simple and efficient procedure would involve:

— Time/date stamp all mail as soon as is received.

— Record in the mail register (a book to record all mail received and sent).

— Sort into appropriate batches—internal and guest.

— Distribute promptly.

Guest mail dealing

Guest mail may fall into four categories and therefore it is important to know how to handle each type efficiently. The following procedures are suggested:

— Mail for guests in residence

  — Sort alphabetically.

  — Check against the alphabetical guest list and write the room number on the envelope.

  — Place in the appropriate pigeonhole in the letter rack. Large envelopes, packages, and registered mail will need to be stored in a separate place.

  — Notification may be sent to the guest to tell him that mail has arrived, for example, if the hotel has a telephone message light system this might be activated.

  — Alternatively, the hotel may operate a delivery system where standard mail is delivered to the guest room by the porter/bellboy.

  — A notification memo is placed in the pigeonhole in the letter rack asking the guest to collect it if a

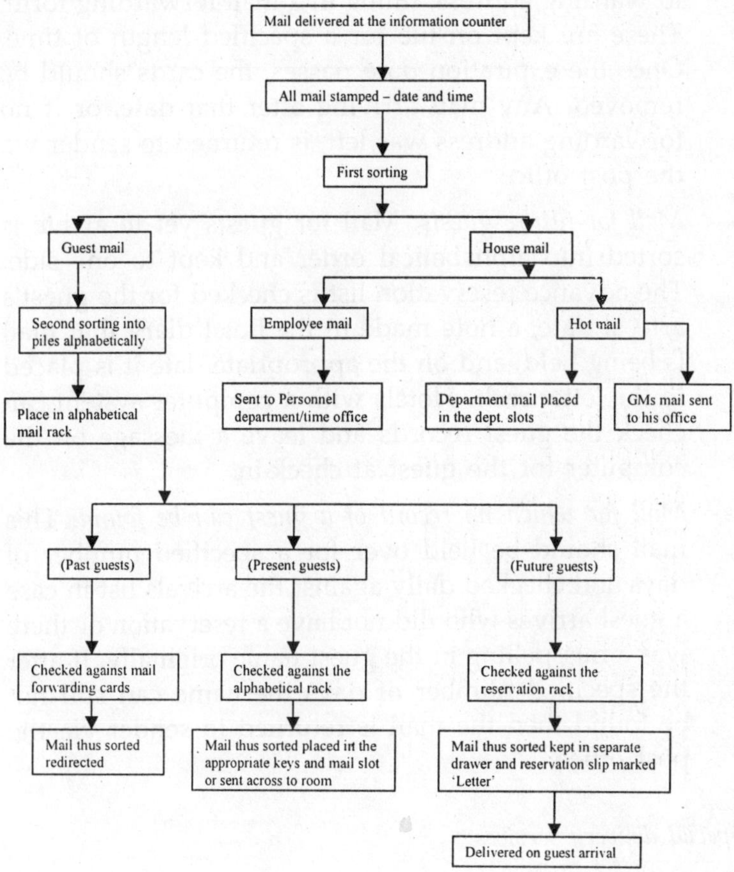

Figure 1. Handling of mail at the information counter

registered letter or package is received at the reception or information desk.

- *Mail for departed guests*: Many guests will leave a forwarding address, filling in a mail forwarding form. These are kept on file for a specified length of time. Once the expiration date passes, the cards should be removed. Any mail arriving after that date, or if no forwarding address was left, is returned to sender via the post office.
- *Mail for future guests*: Mail for guests yet to arrive is sorted into alphabetical order and kept to one side. The advance reservation list is checked for the guest's arrival date, a note made in the hotel diary that mail is being held, and on the appropriate date it is placed in the letter rack. Hotels with a computer system can check the guest records and leave a message on the computer for the guest at check-in.
- *Mail for which no record of a guest can be found*: This mail should be held over for a specified number of days and checked daily against the arrivals list in case a guest arrives who did not have a reservation or there was a misspelling in the guest name originally. If after the specified number of days the name can still not be found then the mail is returned to sender via the post office.

Special delivery services

Registered mail and special delivery services, for example DHL, must be signed for by the person accepting delivery and in turn must be signed for by the guest on collection. The recommended procedure for handling deliveries of this sort is:

- Enter into a logbook with date, time of arrival, and receipt number

— Place under lock and key or in a safe

— A notification memo is placed in the letter rack or the message light is switched on asking the guest to collect.

— The logbook is signed by the guest to confirm that they have taken delivery

However, you should always check the hotel policy and procedure regarding this and follow the guidelines accordingly.

Dealing with outgoing mail

If reception is responsible for dealing with any outgoing mail then a procedure is necessary to ensure that this mail is dispatched with the minimum delay. A standard procedure might be:

— Set a deadline for receipt of mail to be mailed that day.

— Make regular collections from the various departments throughout the day.

— Sort and weigh to ensure the correct postage is affixed.

— Post office receipts for registered mail should be attached in a special book kept for that purpose.

Messages Handling Procedure

Messages are normally conveyed in writing or verbally. Many of which will need to be passed on by the receptionist to another person who may be:

— A member of staff

— A customer, guest, conference delegate, visitor, friend, relative or colleague of a customer

— A potential customer

If you receive a message for someone else verbally it is always a good idea to write it down rather than pass it on verbally, especially if the message is complicated or the person to receive it is not available straight away.

Written messages

- Are permanent
- Are more likely to be accurate
- Ensure you don't forget details
- Can be referred to later

Verbal message

- May never be passed on
- May get distorted in the telling
- May miss out important facts
- Are difficult to check for accuracy

Procedure for taking messages

- Establish who the message is for
- Write message down accurately with all the relevant details:
    - Make sure the facts are correct
    - Think what the recipient needs to know
    - Be concise

The most common mistakes when taking down messages over the phone are:

- Missing out a figure from a telephone number
- Forgetting to ask the caller's name
- Not taking the callers telephone number

- Repeat the message back to caller

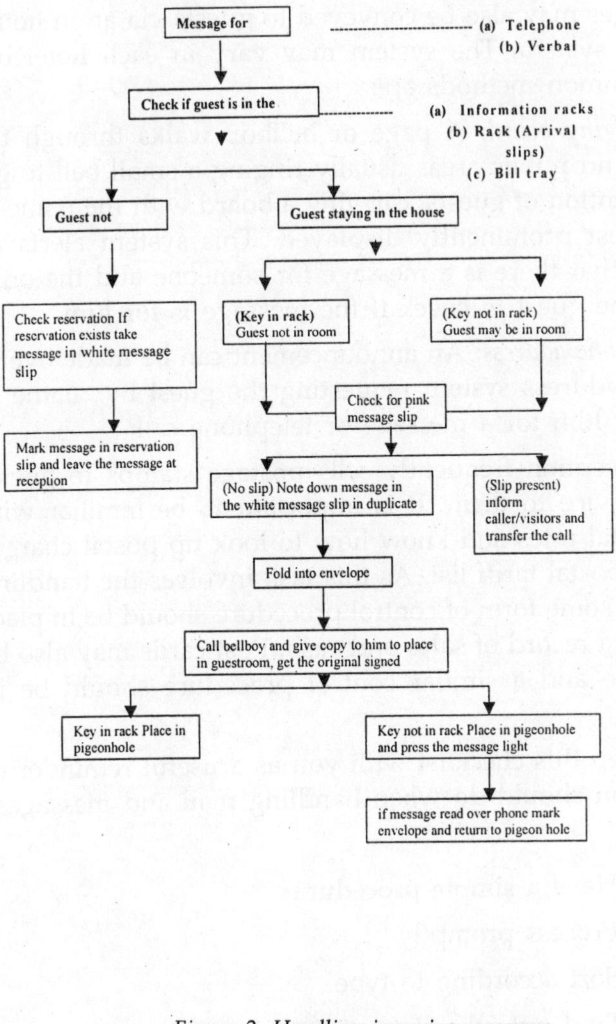

Figure 2. Handling incoming messages

— Pass on the message immediately or as soon as possible.

— Check if possible that the recipient has understood.

Conveying messages

Messages may also be conveyed to guests via an in-house paging system. The system may vary in each hotel but the common methods are:

Paging board: A page or bellboy walks through the lobby and public areas usually ringing a small bell to get the attention of guests, carrying a board with the name of the guest prominently displayed. This system alerts all guests that there is a message for someone and the onus is on the guest to check if the message is for him.

Public address: An announcement can be made over a public address system requesting the guest by name to identify him for a message or telephone call.

Reception frequently sells postage stamps to guests as a service to them. It is important to be familiar with the postal rates and know how to look up postal charges on the postal tariff list. As this task involves the handling of cash, some form of control procedure should be in place to keep a record of sales and cash. Post cards may also be available and a similar control procedure should be in place.

Keep this checklist with you as a useful reminder of what you should do when handling mail and messages.

— *Do:*

  — Have a simple procedure

  — Process promptly

  — Sort according to type

  — Find out who the recipient is

- — Know where to direct it
- — Record it if necessary
- — Check for accuracy
- — Distribute without delay
- — Be afraid to ask… "What goes where and who gets what>"

— *Don't:*

- — Let everything pile up
- — Be disorganised
- — Delay

3

FRONT OFFICE ACCOUNTING

The front office accounting system is responsible for:

— Creating and maintaining an accurate accounting record for each guest or non-guest in the hotel

— Tracking all financial transactions throughout the guest cycle

— Ensuring internal control over cash and non-cash transactions

— Recording settlement for all goods & services provided

The front office accounting system shall be customised and tailored to track each hotel's needs. Therefore, no two hotels have exactly the same front office accounting systems.

Generally Accepted Accounting Principles (GAAP) are the following:

— *Unit of Measurement*: Companies operating in a specific country shall use that country's local currency as a unit of measurement.

— *Historical Cost*: The principle of historical cost states that the value of merchandise or services obtained through business transactions should be recorded in terms of actual costs, not current market values.

— *Going Concern*: The principle of going concern (also known as continuity of the business unit) requires financial statement to be prepared under the assumption that the business will continue indefinitely and thus carry out its commitments. Normally, a business is assumed to be a going concern unless there is objective evidence to the contrary.

— *Conservatism*: The principle of conservatism guides the decisions of accountants in areas that involve estimates and other areas that may call for professional judgement. Therefore, the principle of conservatism provides accountants with a practical alternative for situations that involve doubt. In these very situations, the solution or method shall be the one that does not overstate assets or income.

— *Objectivity*: This very principle states that all business transactions must be supported by objective evidence proving that the transactions did in fact occur.

— *Realisation*: Under the realisation principle, revenues resulting from business transactions are recorded only when a sale has been made and earned, when a hotel receives cash from a guest served in the dining room, for example.

— *Matching*: The matching principle states that all expenses must be recorded in the same accounting period as the revenue that they helped to generate. When expenses are matched with the revenue they helped to produce, external and internal users of financial statements can make better judgements about the financial position and operating performance of the hospitality business. There are two accounting methods for determining when to record results of a business transaction: cash accounting and accrual accounting.

— *Consistency*: The generally accepted accounting principle of consistency states that, once an accounting method has been adopted, it should be followed consistently from period to period. This way, accounting information can be comparable.

Accounting Terminologies

Some accounting terminologies used frequently in the front office department are given below:

Accounts: An Account is a form on which financial data are accumulated, summarised and brought to its ending balance. Moreover, all accounts shall have two entries referred to as Debit (dr) (or charges) versus Credit (cr) (or payments). The most widely used representation of accounts is the T-Account, which summarises debit entries on the left-hand side and credit entries on the right-hand side.

Hotels operating under the manual system get use of journal forms to account for different front office accounting transactions. As far as front office accounting is concerned, there are two major types of accounts widely used:

— Guest accounts describe all charges and payments of guests who are already registered at the hotel.

— Non-guest (house or city) accounts: describe all charges and payments of non-guests. To illustrate, a potential guest sending a certain deposit to guarantee a reservation is a non-guest. Moreover, charges and payments of guests who checkout with any method of payment other than cash, shall be opened a non-guest account. Lastly, visitors and employees with charge privileges shall be opened non-guest accounts.

Folios: A folio is a statement of all transactions (i.e. debits & credits) affecting the balance of a single account. At

Checkout, any guest folio should be balanced to 0 through full cash payment, credit card transfer, personal check transfer, special programme transfer, and direct billing transfer.

The correct way of maintaining folios starts with proper posting, which is the process of recording transactions on a folio (i.e. proper folio, proper location and proper amount). Under the manual, semi automated and fully automated systems, folios are called hand-written folios, machine-posted folios, and computer-based electronic folios respectively. Moreover, all folios shall have a unique serial number for internal control and storing purposes. In the front office department, there are four common types of folios used:

— *Guest folios*: accounts assigned to individual persons or guestrooms

— *Master Folios*: accounts assigned to more than one person or guest room; usually reserved for guest groups

— *Non-Guest (or semi-permanent) folios*: accounts assigned to non-guest businesses or agencies with hotel charge purchase privileges

— *Employee Folios*: accounts assigned to employees with charge purchase privileges

Apart from the above mentioned common folios, front office department get use of some other types of folios such as A-type, B-type, C-type, D-type, and E-type folios.

Vouchers: Vouchers depict the details of the transaction information gathered at the source of transaction and is, hence, a supporting documents used only for internal control purposes. Below are some of the commonly used vouchers in the hospitality industry:

— Cash vouchers

— Credit card vouchers

— Charge vouchers
— Transfer vouchers
— Paid-out vouchers
— Correction vouchers
— Allowance vouchers

Points of sale [POS]: A point of sale is the location at which goods or services are purchased; sometimes called a revenue center. Moreover, due to technology breakthrough, some non-traditional point of sales emerged such as in-room movie and in-room vending service systems. Since charges are usually incurred at remote points of sale, and guest and non-guest folios are maintained at the front office department, posting of different guest and non-guest charges shall be performed. An electronic transfer ensures this, under the fully automated system. Under manual and semi automated systems posting shall be done by a physical submission of different vouchers to the front office department.

When posting charges, the following items shall be considered:

— Amount of the charge
— Name of the point of sales outlet
— Room number & name of the guest
— Brief description of the charge
— Guest signature & employee identification

Ledgers: The front office ledger is the collection of front office account folios, which usually include guest ledgers (i.e. charges and payments of all guests staying at the hotel). At any moment in time, the account receivable includes the addition of guest ledger and non-guest ledger (or city ledger) which refers to charges and payments of all non-guests.

Creation and Maintenance of Guest Accounts

All guest folios shall be created during the pre-arrival or arrival stage of the guest cycle. Moreover, folios might be either placed in front desk folio tray [i.e. posting tray, folio well, or bucket] or stored as an electronic guest folios in fully automated systems. As far as walk-ins are concerned, all their guest folios are created at the arrival stage!

Record keeping systems:

— *Non- automated systems*: Ensured through a series of columns listing individual debit and credit entries accumulated during the occupancy stage after which and establishment of an ending outstanding balance is needed.

— *Semi-automated systems*: Under this very system, all guest transactions should be printed sequentially on a machine-posted folio. Later, the front office clerk needs to come up with the folio outstanding balance. It is extremely important here to mention that, under this very system, each account's previous balance shall be re-entered each time a transaction is posted to the folio.

— *Fully-automated systems*: All guest charges are automatically posted to an electronic folio

Guest charge privileges: Potential guests who would like to have guest charge privileges shall present an imprint of an acceptable credit card or direct billing authorisation at registration. Failing to do so, guests would have to pay, in full, all their charges through cash, hence called Paid-in-Advance [PIA] guests and have, hence, have no post status.

Credit monitoring: In order to monitor and control charge privileges, the front office clerk should check whether the total net purchases are less than the minimum of floor Limit (i.e.: credit card company's limit) and house limit (i.e. hotel's limit). At least, each day, lists of guests with high risk or high balance accounts shall be communicated to all point of sale outlets. This is vital since, failing to do so, will let point of sales outlets continue giving charge privileges to a point that eventually the credit card company refuses to pay the amount of money exceeding its limit. This will cause very serious financial losses to the hotel.

Account maintenance: Whatsoever system hotels operate, maintenance of guest and non-guest accounts is ensured by the following formula:

Net outstanding balance = Previous balance + Debits — Credits

NOB = PB + DR — CR

Tracking Transactions

Under the manual and semi-automated systems, tracking transactions is ensured through an intensive use of vouchers. On the other hand, Under fully automated systems, tracking transactions is ensured through on-line electronic transfer of transactional information from remote points of sale to the front office main frame terminal.

In accounting, a transaction is an exchange of goods and services for cash or a promise to pay. Under this very assumption, "nothing happens until a transaction occurs". This means that front office clerks shall first of all have a transaction, its supporting documents to be able later to debit or credit certain accounts. In hotels transactions might have the form of:

— *Cash payment*: In this very transaction, front office clerks shall post cash payment as a credit in the guest folio. Moreover, cash vouchers shall be used as a transaction-supporting document.

— *Charge purchase*: Charge purchases represent deferred payment transactions that increase the outstanding balance of a folio account. In this transaction type, front office clerks shall use charge vouchers as a transaction-supporting document.

— *Account correction*: Account correction is used to resolve a posting error in a folio detected at the day the error is made (i.e. before the closing of the business day). In this transaction, front office clerks shall use correction vouchers as a transaction-supporting document.

— *Account allowance*: Account allowances occur because of two reasons:

  — Either as compensation of poor service, or as rebates for coupon discounts. That way, guest outstanding balance decreases.

  — As to correct a posting error detected after the closing of the business day.

For both reasons, front office clerks shall prepare an allowance voucher as a transaction supporting document.

— Current transfer

— Cash advance

Internal Control

In the hotel industry, the main purpose of internal control is to track transaction documentation, verify account entries and account balances, and to identify vulnerabilities in the accounting system. The keyword to internal control is auditing, which is the process of verifying front office accounting records for accuracy and completeness. Below are some forms that are of extreme importance to internally control, one of the most vital assets in the hotel (i.e. cash):

— *Front office cash sheet*: The front office cash sheet lists each cash receipt or disbursement in order to reconcile cash on hand at the end of a cashier's shift with the documented transaction that occurred during the same shift.

— *Cash, house banks or petty cash*: Petty cash is the amount of cash assigned to a cashier so that he/she can handle the various transactions that occur in a particular work shift. At the beginning of each shift, all cashiers must sign their cash banks and at the end of the shift, shall deposit all cash, checks, and other negotiable instruments in the general cashier's safe deposit box. Moreover, at the end of each shift, cashiers should watch out for cash discrepancies (i.e. any difference between front office cash sheet and the actual amounts in their cash drawers).

  Cash discrepancies might have the form of cash overages, shortages, or due backs. Lastly, cashiers might come up with the net cash receipt, which is: Amount of all cash, checks, and other negotiable instruments in cashier's drawer—amount of the initial cash bank + all paid outs

— *Audit control*: Along with the fact that hotels might employ internal control auditors, at least once in a year, (especially for hotels traded in the stock market) to get use of external certified public accountants responsible for approving hotel's accounts.

Internal Control for Food and Beverage Sales:

Guest Check (also called Server's Checks): This initiates the Food & Beverage order taken from the guest, and represents the invoice given to the guest.

— Guest checks should be pre-numbered, tinted and have duplicates. Moreover, it shall be kept in locked storage, in numerical order.

— Used checks, unused checks versus void checks!
— Post to dinner, the server must price and total the guest check (applicable for manual systems), unless the point-of-sale equipment can automatically perform the addition.
— Later, the cashier receives payment or makes the guest sign his/her guest check and deposits everything to the cashier.
— At the end of the shift, the cashier's cash drawer and supporting documents are accounted for (i.e. cash, credit card vouchers, food charges, and any miscellaneous paid-outs). Later, they are reconciled against cash register reading using a daily cashier's report
— Beverage sales in a lounge, a bar presents a harder job for internal control
— Some basic internal control procedures for beverage sales are listed as follows:
    — Require the bartender to ring each sale as it is made
    — Require the bartender to insert each paid check into a locked box
    — The cash register drawer shall never remain open even for a small period of time
    — Servers are not allowed to first pay the bartender in cash and collect later from customers
    — Bartenders should not be allowed to take register readings or reconcile their own cash at the end of their shifts

Guest charge privileges are allocated to guests who have provided an imprint of a valid credit card or were given a direct billing privilege at registration. In this case, all guest charges are recorded as debits in their respective guest, or master folios.

Accounts Settlement

One of the responsibilities of front office clerks is to settle guest accounts, which means the eventual collection of payment for outstanding account balances (i.e. bringing account balances to 0]. This is usually ensured either by full cash payment, transfer to an approved credit card, personal check, special programme, or direct billing account. Checkout and settlement describe the activities associated with the final stage of the guest cycle (i.e. departure).

The major activities, which are conducted at departure, include:

- Resolving outstanding guest account balances
- Updating room status information
- Creating guest history records

Departure Procedures: At checkout, front office clerks shall:

- Check for mails, messages, and faxes
- Check for safe deposit box, or in-room safe keys
- Post all outstanding charges
- Verify account information
- Inquire about additional recent charges
- Present the guest folio for guest signature
- Verify the method of payment
- Process the account payment (i.e. zeroing out the account)
- Update the room status

Methods of Settlement

- *Full cash payment*: the front office clerk shall destroy the guest's credit card voucher

— *Personal check payment*: the front office clerk shall shift the credit from guest ledger to personal check account, which is a sub-account of the city ledger and the guest shall only sign a personal check voucher

— *Credit card payment*: the front office clerk shall shift the credit from guest ledger to credit card account, which is a sub-account of the city ledger and the guest shall only sign a credit card voucher

— *Special programme payment*: the front office clerk shall shift the credit from guest ledger to special programme account, which is a sub-account of the city ledger and the guest shall only sign a special programme voucher

— *Direct billing payment*: the guest shall sign only his/her folio, and depart. Later, he/she, upon receipt of hotel invoice, shall deposit a certain amount of money in the hotel bank account.

— *Combined settlement method*: In this case, depending on which combination, front office clerk shall proceed by preparing different kinds of vouchers!

Sales minded cashiers: As guests tends to depart from the hotel, the cashiers shall approach them in the following way:

— Provide them comment cards and encourage them to use these very cards

— Thank the guest for choosing the hotel and wish him/her a safe trip

— Ask the guest whether he/she is considering returning to the property on any return trip to the area. Cashiers might sometimes accept future reservations!

Late check out: Late check out refers to the situation where guests check out after the hotel's established check out time. Late check out shall not be considered as a guest right, rather a privilege which might be honoured by the front office manager upon room availability whether free of charge or charged a late check out fee. There are a lot of innovative ways to check out apart from the traditional way. Below are two commonly used check out options (apply usually only to guests who have provided valid credit cards at registration):

— *Express check out*: This is usually convenient for guests who decide to check out very early in the morning. In fact, at night, bellboys (for example) shall slip the guest folio under the expected departed guestroom. When the guest wakes up, he/she shall sign the gust folio, and the credit card voucher, leave the room, give back the room key to the bellboy, and departs.

— *Self check out*: Guests might check out using self check out terminals situated at public areas or in their rooms if in-room check out systems are integrated with front office main frame.

Unpaid Account Balances: Unpaid account balances occur because of the following reasons, most of which are because hotels do not operate fully-automated systems:

— A departing guest honestly forgetting to settle his/her account

— Late charges (being one of the most important reasons)

— Skippers

In order to minimise late charges, front office clerks shall:

— Post transactional vouchers as soon as they arrive at the front desk

— Survey front office equipment, voucher and folio racks for non-posted charges before the front office clerk checks a guest out

— Ask departing guests whether they have incurred any charge purchase or placed long distance telephone calls, which do not appear on their final folio

Account Collection

All unpaid account balances shall be transferred to city ledger accounts, which might have the form of:

— Credit card billing
— Direct billing
— Travel agency accounts
— Bad check accounts
— Skipper accounts
— Disputed bills accounts
— Guaranteed reservation accounts
— Late charge accounts
— House accounts

In order to receive all their city ledger accounts, hotels shall devise effective and efficient account receivables billing procedures. To do so, every property shall try to find answers to the following questions:

— When are outstanding accounts balances payable?
— How many days shall separate each two consecutive invoices?
— How to contact the departed guests whose accounts is not yet paid?

After coming with answers to the above mentioned questions, hotels, then, shall depending on the amount of money to be collected, and the geographical distance that separates the hotel from the guest billing address, opt for one of the following collection schedules:

— Aggressive (short cycle) collection schedule
— Lenient (long cycle) collection schedule

Account Aging

Account aging refers to the method(s) of tracking past due

accounts based on the dates the charges were incurred. To illustrate, credit card payment accounts usually have ages of maximum one month. However, some other non-guest accounts (ex. late charges, disputed bills, bad checks and skippers accounts) might have ages measured in months, and even years. Below, is the terminology associated with each account age:

— Less than 30 days accounts—Current Accounts

— More than 30 days accounts—Overdue Accounts

— Older than 90 days accounts—Delinquent Accounts

Guidelines for Cashiers

— The opening machine totals for paid and paid-out must be the same figures that appear on the previous shift's cash report as the closing machine totals for paid and paid-out

— At the close of the shift, the cashier should subtotal paid and paid-out for the current shift, and record the closing figures in the machine's totals column

— If at any stage, cashier accidentally miss-keys any transaction, adjustments can be made to the machine

— Net cash received = cash paid-in (closing)—cash paid-in (beginning)

— Net cash paid-out = cash paid-out (closing)—cash paid-out (beginning)

— Net cash sum of cashier's shift = net cash received—net cash paid-out

— The cashier should extract the net cash sum from the cash drawer, and secure the money in the general cashier's safe deposit box until deposited in the Bank

— At the end of any shift, the cash drawer should contain exactly the same amount as it did when the cashier opened his/her shift.

— If any cash overage or shortage occur, the cashier must recheck the cash report and search all the transaction records for possible miss-keyed entries

Hotel Expense Accounting

In the accounting terminology, expense is an income statement account representing the cost of items consumed in the process of generating revenue or that expires due to the passage of time. Expense cannot be mixed with expenditure. For, Expenditure represents the purchase amount of a certain asset. In the hotel industry, expenses are divided into two main categories:

Direct expenses

These are the expenses that vary with the level of production. For example, in the Food and Beverage department, the Cost of Food Sales is a direct expense. For, the more dishes we serve, the more cost of Food Sales the Hotel incurs. Moreover, in the Telephone Department, the Cost of Calls is a direct expense. For, the more we connect guests to whatever destination wanted, the more cost of calls the hotel incurs. At this very stage a bracket would be opened to explain that there is a primordial difference between revenue generator departments.

In fact, revenue generator departments are classified into two: Service Type departments versus merchandising departments. Service type departments are revenue generators making money from solely providing services (Ex. Rooms Division department). On the other hand, merchandising departments ensure revenue by getting use of certain raw material, processing it, and than sell the final product. Therefore, only merchandising departments have a direct expense called Cost of Sales.

Indirect expenses

These are the expenses that do not vary with the level of production, or variable costs that can not be feasibly distributed to various Financial Reporting Centers. In the hotel industry, indirect expenses are, hence, divided into two different categories:

Fixed Charges: Examples might include rent, insurance, property taxes, and interest expense. For, these very expenses are incurred for the benefit of the hotel as a whole not for the benefit of each single department. To illustrate, if a hotel insures itself against fire, theft and burglary, and one day some valuable equipment has been stolen, from any department whatsoever, the insurance company will indemnify the hotel.

Undistributed Expenses: Examples might include electricity, energy, and water expenses. For, usually the hotel receives a total energy bill to be paid. In the old days, some hotels went for allocating this amount according to certain factors. However, this practice proved to be misleading, since it might under-allocate energy expenses for some departments and over-allocate it for others. Nowadays, most of the hotels decide not to allocate such expenses any more. Rather, hotels report such expenses in separate schedules.

At this stage, departments of a typical hotel would be listed along with their various related direct expenses. Later, examples of fixed charges and undistributed expenses would be discussed. Last, a bracket would be opened to discuss one of the most important Direct Expenses in any hotel, which is Payroll and Related Expenses. For, hotels being described as labour intensive companies devote a big percentage of their financial resources to such an expense.

Typical hotel departments

Rooms Division Department: It is the place where guests receive several kinds of services ranging from reservation, registration, to checkout and settlement of their accounts. This department typically compromises a Rooms Division manager, an assistant manager(s), registration clerks, cashiers, mail and information clerk, and uniform service personnel. The various types of Rooms Division department direct expenses include:

— *Commissions expenses*: This account includes payments by the hotel to authorised agents that bring room business to the hotel. Usually at the end of each month, hotels sit with these agents in order to reconcile their monthly sales figures and authorise commission payment (usually in the form of a percentage of room revenue)

— *Reservation expenses*: This expense account represents any payment to various agents contracting to bring potential room revenue business to the hotel. These agents might have the form of Central Reservation Offices (Whether affiliate or non-affiliate), Intersell agencies.

— *Contract cleaning expenses*: This expense account represents payment to contracting outside cleaning agencies. Some hotels (especially small and middle size hotels) might opt for contract cleaning because of its attractive financial implications. If this is the case, these hotels might not be forced to have a housekeeping department, or might keep housekeeping staff to minimum. Such expenses should be determined in light of the contract signed between both parties (i.e. the hotel from one side and the cleaning company from the other.)

— *Laundry and dry cleaning expenses*: This cost applies to outside laundry and dry cleaning costs for the Rooms

Division department. In most of the cases, such contracts are signed to benefit more than one revenue generator. In this case, the rooms division department shall report the laundry and dry cleaning expenses related only to the Rooms Division department.

- *Guest transportation expenses*: These expenses include the cost of transporting guests from and to the hotel via various means of transportation (ex: Mini-buses, limousines.). If the guest transportation's volume business, staff, and costs are significantly high, then a separate department might be established.
- *Linen expenses*: This specific expense account includes the allocation of a portion of linen expenditure for a specific period of time. This practice goes along with one of the accounting principles: the matching principle. Some sub-accounts of linen expense might be:
  - Towels expenses
  - Blankets expenses
  - Facecloth expenses
  - heets expenses
  - Pillow expenses
- *Guest supplies expenses*: This account includes the various guest supplies provided free of charge to guests in their rooms. Some sub-accounts of guest supplies expenses might include:
  - Newspaper expenses
  - Guest stationary expenses
  - Shoe cloth expenses
  - Coffee expenses
  - Writing supplies expenses
  - Toilet requisites expenses

- Flowers expenses
- Hangers expenses
- Matches expenses
- Ice expenses
- Candy expenses

— *Cleaning supplies expenses*: Such an account includes the cost of Rooms Division's cleaning supplies. Some sub-accounts of guest supplies expenses might include:

- Brooms expenses
- Soaps and polishes expenses
- Cleaning cloths expenses
- Mops expenses
- Cleaning chemicals expenses
- Dusters expenses
- Brushes expenses
- Insecticides expenses
- Dustpans expenses
- Pail expenses
- Disinfectants expenses
- Cleaning accessories expense

— *Printing and stationary expenses*: This expense account includes printed formats, office supplies, printed manuals and guidelines for the use of the Rooms Division employees. Some sub-accounts of printing and stationary expenses might include:

- Binders expenses
- Floor plans expenses
- Pencils and Pens expenses
- Vouchers expenses
- Rack card expenses

— Reports expenses
— Desk pad expenses
— Envelopes expenses
— Ink expenses
— Folio expenses

— *Uniforms expenses*: This expense account includes the allocation of a portion of uniforms asset (if the hotel purchases uniforms) for a certain period of time along with the expense of repairing, and cleaning them. If the hotel rents uniforms rather than purchasing them, then the uniform expense shall include the renting cost, usually predetermined in light of the contract linking the hotel and the uniform renting company.

Food & Beverage Department: This department is responsible for the preparation and service of food and beverage to guests. It compromises the kitchen, restaurants, bars, and any premise in which Food and Beverage is served.

Telephone Department: This department is responsible to handle guest communication. This might be insured through connecting guests to desired locations, whether in-house, local or long distance calls. Moreover, this department is usually composed of a chief operator, supervisors, operators, and messengers. Last, with the automation revolution affecting right now most hotels, it became possible to separate calls of guests and communication handled by hotel employees, therefore, making it possible to have the telephone department as a minor revenue generating department. For, prior to automation, the separation of cost of calls was not possible and hence the telephone department might show frequently a loss since telephone direct costs are overstated.

Administrative & General Department: Actually looking at any hotel organisation chart, Administrative and

General Department (A&G) does not exist. It is however a financial reporting centers including executives of the Hotel and other employees involved with executive and financial activities (ex: Accounting personnel, resident Manager, Accounts Receivable clerks, Night Auditors). Moreover, if there is staff in the hotel not included in departments due to low business volume not justifying the establishment of a department, they might be included under the A& G department (ex. Data Processing Staff, Transportation Staff, and Personnel Staff).

Marketing Department: This department is composed of a marketing manager, marketing assistant managers responsible for sales, convention, public relations, and advertising functions, along with marketing personnel. This department is a cost center that indirectly supports revenue generators in their sole aim of generating hotel revenue. This can be insured, for example, through large group reservations, hence maximising room revenue, or buffet, conference, and catering opportunities brought by this very department hence maximising room revenue, F& B revenue, and the hotel revenue as a whole.

Property, Operation and Maintenance (POM): Concerned with the appearance and physical condition of the building, the repair and maintenance of equipment, and rubbish removal. Some positions of this department might include POM manager, POM assistant manager(s), electricians, plumbers, gardeners, painters, and interior design specialists.

Data Processing Department: This special department might be established in hotels operating under the fully automated system. Moreover, such hotels should have significant investment in computer equipment and staff to justify the establishment of a single department. If these conditions do not exist, than the Data Processing functions would be financially grouped under administrative & general department.

Human Resources Department: Similar to data processing department, if the dollar amount and staff incurred for employees' hiring, screening, interviewing, selecting, recruiting, and Training is significant, than a human resources department may be established. Otherwise, human resources functions would be financially grouped under administrative & general department

Guest Transportation Department: If the dollar amount and Number of Staff employed in the transportation of Guests is significant, a separate department might be established. Otherwise, guest transportation staff would be grouped under rooms division department.

Financial reporting center

A financial reporting center is an area of responsibility for which separate cost information must be collected, might be classified as revenue centers, support centers, and other financial reporting centers

Revenue Centers—Generate revenue through sales of Products and/or services to guests

— Rooms

— Food and Beverage

— Telephone

— Gift Shops

— Garage and Parking

— Other Operated Departments

— Rentals and other Income

Support Centers—those departments that have minimal guest contact and do not produce Sales. Yet, they do provide services to revenue centers, which, in turn, provide services to guests

— Administrative & General
— Marketing
— Property Operation and Maintenance
— Data Processing
— Human Resources

Other Financial Reporting Centers—include Energy Costs and Fixed Charges (Rent Expense, Property Taxes, Insurance Expense, Interest Expense, Depreciation and Amortisation Expenses)

Front Office Records

The major two front office records that are stored at departure are guest history records (which are stored alphabetically) and guest folios (stored numerically)

Guest History Records

Guest history records are collections of personal & financial data about guests who have stayed at the hotel. Maintaining guest history records helps the hotel better understand its clientele and determine guest trends when they develop. Moreover, these very records might serve as a source of mailing list or to identify guest characteristics that are important to strategic marketing. In addition, they serve as to develop and place advertisements that appeal to the types of clientele the hotel attempts to attract. Finally guest history records points out the need for a new, supplementary, or enhanced services.

Moreover, even though guest history records are stored in the front office department, they are handed to marketing department, whenever needed. In fact, marketing department might get use of guest history records as to create a programme to reward frequent guests with a free stay after a certain number of visits, or as an indicator to watch out for future repeat guest reservations in order to increase the hotel's repeat business market share. Guests tend to remember the friendliness, convenience, and special services that distinguish one property from another. This is called competitive advantage.

Night Audit

The major functions of the night audit is to:

— Verify posted entries to guest and non-guest accounts

— Balance all front office accounts

— Resolve room status and rate discrepancies

— Monitor guest credit limits

— Produce operational and managerial reports

The night audit requires attention to accounting detail, procedural controls, and guest credit restrictions. In this sense, the night auditor shall track room revenues, occupancy percentages, and other standard operating statistics. He/she shall, also, prepare a daily summary of cash, check, and credit card activities that occurred in the front office department on a daily basis. In night auditing, end of the business day is a vital time for the auditor. As far as the closing of business day is concerned, management shall determine the end of day, which is the time after which the night audit can prepare his/her daily Reports. This end of day is usually the time where the majority of outlets close or no more have frequent activity.

The night auditor shall always compare the data conveyed in different folios against points of sales outlets daily reports, housekeeping room status report. This is called cross-referencing, and is a vital procedure in the internal control. After comparing, the night auditor should come up with the guest, non-guest, and departmental accounts. This total should match the daily POS totals (i.e. in balance). If not, then the auditor is said to be out-of-balance, and the night auditor shall substantially review all account statements, vouchers, support documents, and departmental source of documentation in order to bring the audit to balance.

The night audit shall compare all credit limits of guests and non-guests accounts with credit card floor limits, hotel's house limit, guest's status and reputation. If high balance accounts are detected, the night auditor shall note and report this to management the following day. Under the manual, a daily transcript and a supplementary transcript are used to track daily transactions of guest and non-guest accounts respectively. Hotels operating under semi-automated systems use D-Cards for the same purpose.

Non-automated system: under this very system, 4 forms are widely used, which are:

— Daily and supplementary transcripts
— Guest and non-Guest folios
— Front office cash sheets

Semi-automated system: The audit of guest and non-guest accounts is ensured mostly through mechanical or electronic posting machines. The most important form obtained under this very system is the D Card.

Fully-automated system: This very system is the best compared to manual and semi-automated systems. In fact, this system can be interfaced with point of sale terminals, call accounting systems, and other revenue centers for quick, accurate and automatic postings to electronic guest and non-guest account folios. This very fact enables the night auditor to concentrate more on auditing transactions and analysing front office activities.

Night Audit Process: The night audit process focuses on two areas:

— Discovery and correction of front office accounting errors ensured through the cross-referencing process.
— Creation of accounting and managerial reports including audit balance, average rate, occupancy percentage, usage of package plans and other marketing programmes, and the number of group rooms and complementary rooms occupied.

The main steps of the night audit process are:

— Complete outstanding posting
— Reconcile room status discrepancies
— Verify room rates
— Balance all departmental accounts
— Verify no-show reservations
— Post room rates and taxes
— Prepare required reports
— Prepare cash receipts for deposit
— Clear or back up the system
— Distribute reports

Most of the errors encountered in the night audit process stem from the fact that the hotel is not operating under fully automated system. The widely occurring errors in the night audit process can have the form of:

— Pickup errors
— Transposition errors
— Missing folios

In short, night auditor must be:

— Responsible for entering all room charges, separating room taxes from room revenues and insuring that all vouchers have been accounted for and properly posted to each guest folio.

— Prepare the front office room status report and reconcile it with the housekeeper's report for any room discrepancy

— Verify Food & Beverage charges made to guests and charged to their rooms with the daily Food and Beverage sales reports. This duty is conducted, also, for all other revenue centers.

— Guest folio errors (whether overcharges or undercharges) shall be corrected by the night auditor using either a correction or an allowance voucher and posted to a separate allowance journal.

— Responsible for preparing a summary report of the up-to-date amounts owned to the hotel in both guest ledger and city ledger accounts

4

FRONT OFFICE COMMUNICATION

Conversation must be a matter of equal give and take, but unhappily it is frequently all "Take". The voluble speaker monopolises the conversation without giving anyone else a chance to do any thing but to wait for a chance that never seems to come. There is a simple way by which one who is inclined to run-on can refrain himself from being a pest or a pest a bore: stop and think.

Compliments: We all love to receive compliments and tend to love those who offer them. Yet it is a wonder why so few people give them. It may some time be due to an aversion to being too personal or due to shyness or embarrassment. If you are the one being complimented don't simper or belittle whatever the compliment referred to. The appropriate way to respond to any compliment is to say "thank you", or "I am so glad you like it".

Personal Remarks: Compliments and other favorable personal remarks are not only permissible but also desirable. But unpleasant remarks, or remarks that make another person uncomfortable, are definitely in bad taste. The old adage " If you can't say something nice, don't say anything at all" is very good advice.

Uunkind Remarks: Conversation should never be about someone else, especially in a group, even a group of close friends. No matter how tempted you are to pass a nasty comment or to join in a group talking unkindly about another, don't do it. It doesn't just defame the character of the other it also makes you look bad.

Using Tact: If you find another's opinion totally unacceptable, try to change the subject as soon as possible. If you care too intensely about a subject, it is dangerous to allow yourself to say anything. If you are able to listen with an open mind, you may safely speak on any topic. After all, any mutually interesting topic may lead to one about which you don't agree. It is better to withdraw unless you can argue without bitterness or bigotry.

The Bore: One definition of a bore is "one who talks about himself when you want to talk about yourself." This is superficially true, but a bore might more accurately be described as one who insists on telling you at length something that you don't want to hear about at all. He insists that you listen to the bitter end in spite of your obvious boredom.

The Wailer: One of the fundamental and common sense rules of all conversation is that you talk about things that will be interesting and agreeable to the listener. It is unbelievable; therefore that so many people dwell on misfortunes, sickness and other unpleasantness. Don't dwell on your own problems. Your audience has them too and won't be entertained by yours.

The Story Snatcher: We all know people who can't let anyone tell a story to the end. They must jump in and correct the details and finish the story. This is habit that is particularly annoying if it happens frequently. If after a gentle hint from you the time with, ' All right, you tell it. This will stop all but the thickestskinned story-snatcher.

The secert Teller: Another social pariah is the one who, when part of a group, is constantly whispering or talking in low asides to one person alone. The others cannot fail to feel that either the whisperer is talking about them or that they are missing out on some juicy titbit. This also applies to speaking a foreign language that most of the group does not know. It is exactly like a secret and is equally rude.

Corrections: When a person pronounces a word incorrectly, or makes a grammatical error, don't correct him or her, but when the opportunity arises, use the same word or phrase correctly and hope that the mistake will be recognised.

COMMUNICATION ON THE TELEPHONE

The telephone has virtually replaced all other forms of communication and with the frequency of it's use, has come the frequency of it's abuse. One can be held captive on the telephone as easily as in person by a garrulous friend or associate.

Personal Calls: When you talk on the telephone, whether in your home or in an office, the quality of your voice and your ability to express yourself clearly and concisely are of utmost importance. The person at the other end of the line obviously cannot see your facial expressions or gestures, and the impression received depends totally on your voice. Speak clearly and distinctly, with the same inflections one would use in a face-to-face conversation. If you must put the telephone down during the conversation, do it gently, and when you hang up, do not slam the receiver down. The person at the other end may still have the phone close to his ear, and the sudden sharp bang can be quite deafening.

Invitations: Don't let too young a child answer the telephone. A lot of the caller's time is wasted trying to make the child understand the message and relay it back to the right person. Don't hang up before letting the phone ring at least six times. Nothing is more irritating than to rush down form the attic or the bathtub to answer and to find that the caller has hung up.

There are no rules about what you say to friend when you call to invite him or her for a part, but there are couple of things you should consider. You should never start out by saying, "Hi, Mary. What are you doing Saturday night?" or "Are you busy Sunday night?" This man oeuvre puts Mary in the embarrassing position of saying "Nothing" and then not being able to refuse after being told that she is being asked to dine with the Borings or to play golf with the Shanks. On the other hand, if she answers, "I have an engagement" and is then told that she would have been invited to something she likes very much, it is disappointing to be unable to go. A young woman says she is "Busy" and is then told, "Too bad you can't come, because John Brilliant was looking forward to meeting you," cannot change her mind and say, "oh, then I'll get out of my dinner somehow and come." To do so would be thoroughly rude to everyone concerned.

Four Important Don'ts

When you get a number wrong, don't ask, "What number is this?" Ask instead, "is this 555-3456?" so that you can look it up again or dial more carefully the next time. Don't answer the call and then say "Wait a minute" and keep the caller waiting while you vanish on an errand of your own, say instead, "I'll call you back in a few minutes," and do so.

Ansering Machines

These are a great convenience enabling the caller to leave a brief message and let the owner of the machine know who is trying to teach him. The one with the machine should make every effort to make his message brief. A long and rambling message can be both irritating and costly for the long distance caller. The one obligation attached to an answering machine is that you indeed return calls when messages are left.

Call waiting: As convenient as it is to have call waiting, it is also an intrusion on the call you are on. Unless you are expecting an urgent call and say so, it is impolite to continually put someone on hold while you answer another call. This is particularly true when you have made the call in the first place.

Beepers

Many professional people wear beepers at all times, including during social events, because they truly must be continually accessible. If the beeper sounds when in the company of other, the wearer should immediately turn it off since the insistent tone can be irritating, the person should then excuse himself, explain that he must make a call in response to the beeper and do so.

Office Telephone Etiquette

Avoid lengthy personal calls in the office. While personal messages are a times unavoidable, both to make and to receive, long chatty conversations are not only out of place but also wasteful of time that belongs to the company, not to the employee. Telephone chatter irritated other people in the office who cannot help overhearing and interrupts the routine of office procedure.

Handling the Difficult Caller

The caller who insThis can be handled with the following response, "I'm sorry but Ms. Rogers does not speak with people unknown to her until she is aware of the purpose of their call," The caller with a request above and beyond the normal, asking for an employee's phone number, for instance. You should explain, "I am sorry buy I am not privileged to give you that information. Perhaps you could phone her here at their office tomorrow." Whatever the request is do not be coerced into complying with it. The caller referred to you whom you would rather not see or speak to.

Rather than create an issue, you will find it easier to say, "I expect to be terrible busy for the nest few weeks and really will not have time. If you leave your number, I'll try to get back to you after that." The postponement may end the matter. However, if the caller is persistent you may have to se him if you feel obligated to the person who referred him, or if you don't you may cut him off with, "I really haven't time to see you."

The hostile caller. No matter how unfounded his anger you will want to calm him. You might say, "I am terribly sorry if I have done something to make you angry but I cannot help you further in this matter." In the case of service businesses, hostile calls are an every day occurrence. The best way to handle them is. We will do what ever we can to rectify the matter.

Public Telephones

When you are the caller. Be courteous. This is not the time to stack up a pile of quarters and chat with your friends while you wait for an appointment, particularly when there is a line of people waiting to make calls, too. Conduct your business and hang up. If you have a true emergency and are waiting for the telephone behind someone who is going on and on and there are not other pay phone is sight, you may signal to her and state your urgency. She is not obligated to disconnect her call, but should he be willing, it is incumbent upon you to be a quick as possible and return the use of the phone to her.

Tips for Good Conversationalists

- — Show interest in what other people are doing, how they are doing and where they are heading.
- — Are able to make a fast switch, from business to world politics are from ecological concern top a new opera being performed.
- — Know how to tailor their topics to the interest of the people they are addressing. Don't interrupt. It is extremely rude to stop someone in the middle of a discourse, even if he has been dragging on interminably. Wait for a propitious moment, and then break into the conversation, launching another topic.
- — Speak from experience and knowledge and not careless conjecture. Look people straight in the eye when talking to them. Eye contact is important in any situation. If you don't look directly at the person you are talking to, it could mean that you hiding something, or looking for someone more important to talk do. Refrain from correcting in public another person's facts, grammar or pronunciation. Real friends help by pointing out in private, repeated errors that may make a colleague or friend look inarticulate or uneducated.
- — Know how to question a stranger in a friendly, rather than a prying manner.
- — Know when to talk business and when not to. People who can only talk about office matters are usually unmitigated bores. A good conversationalist really contributes to business discussion with peers, associates and clients, but also really contributes to

discussions with people not associated with his business life.

— Don't burst someone's ballooning from of other people. If some one is passionately defending a point of view, it is indefensibly reduce to disagree disagreeably. You can always respond negatively without animosity.

— Address everyone within the group, not just one or two people. It is rude to have the floor and then single out someone to talk to, instead of the group that happens to be present.

It's exclusionary. A good conversationalist catches the eye of each person in the group on a rotating basis while talking, so that every one feels like a partner in the conversation.Know how to make a shy person feel part of the group. If he notices someone off to the side, without anyone to speak to, He will ask that person a question and bring him into the conversation by introducing him and asking his opinion on some matter.

Have a sense of humor. Without it there is no hope of a good conversation or a good rapport.

Correcspondence

In this day of instant electronic mail, computerised desk to desk memos, and the convenience of the telephone a well written letter, personalised stationery, and traditionally and beautifully crafted invitations are truly a pleasure to the recipient. A sincere letter of condolence to a bereaved friend, a formal reply to a formal wedding invitation, a think you notes instead of a commercial thank you card. These are all ways of communicating that are especially meaningful.

Letters

Angry Letters

The light, jesting tone that saves a quip from offense can become sharp and insulting when written. Anger in a letter carries with it the effect of solidified fury. Bitter spoken words fade away once the cause is forgiven; written words are fixed on the page forever. One point canto be overstressed: Letters written under strong emotion should be held for twenty-four and reread before being sent -or probably torn into small pieces and not sent at all.

Thank-you Letters

The most important qualifications of a think you letter are that is sound sincere and that it be written promptly. You use the expressions most natural to you and write as enthusiastically as though you were talking. Insofar as possible, thank-you notes for wedding presents should be written as soon as the gift is received. This is not always possible, but if they are not sent before the wedding, they must be written as soon as the couple returns from their honeymoon.

Your Personal Life

The cardinal principle of etiquette is thoughtfulness, and the guiding rule of thoughtfulness is the golden rule. If you always do unto others as you would have done unto you it is likely that you will never offended, bore or intrude, and that your actions will be courteous and indeed thoughtful.

Ladies First

Over the years society has generally that women are not,

as earlier presumed, frail creatures that can hardly exit their front door without the consul or services of a man to guide them. There is nothing wrong, however, with the continuing customs that allow a man to extend social amenities and instinctive consideration to a woman he is with. Generally, whether it is indoors or outdoors, when walking together the woman precedes the man, through a door or a narrow passage way. But in case they are walking through rough ground the man precedes to help or to assist his lady. He precedes her wherever the lady would require any kind of assistance, as in opening the door, walking down a steep ramp, a slippery stairway etc.

When walking together on a road a man generally walks on the street side of road. If a man is walking with two women at the same time, he should never be sandwiched between the two. Also, a man rarely offers his arm to a woman anymore, unless of course assistance is required. The only other instance when a man offers his arm to a lady is when he is her partner to a formal occasion or he is an usher at a wedding.

Hold a lady by her elbow only when you are to help her into a vehicle or by her hand when leading the way through a crowded area. When going through a door it is customary for the gentlemen to hold the door open for the lady to pass. Traditionally when walking through a revolving door, woman always steps in first when the door is already moving, and when the door is stationary, a man enters first and gets the door moving so that woman may step into the section behind him. When going through a door it is always courteous to hold the door open for the person behind you.

Personal Habits

It would probably be amasing if one could view a videotapes of the various actions that one unconsciously performs as we go about the business of the day. These unconscious acts comprise of all the personal habits that one doesn't even think about, but ideally should. These are some of the things that present an image of who we are to the others and these may be well different from what we may want it to be. Parents play an important role in deciding the future personal habits of their children. People unconsciously do outside, exactly what they have been used to doing at home.

Posture

There is not doubt that a person who sits and walks erect looks the best. Graceful standing and walking posture include: shoulders relaxed, chin in and slightly up, abdomen and stomach in, back straight and knees relaxed. When seated feet are to be on the floor or knees may be crossed. Women in skirts should keep their knees together. Never sprawl onto a chair. Always give room to others.

Chesing Gum

This destroys appearance by chewing gum like a cow chewing cud. Those people who are addicted to chewing gum or those who chew gum because of therapeutic reasons should do so in q quiet and unobtrusive manner. To dispose off a gum it should be carefully wrapped in a paper and thrown into a trash basket.

Smoking in Public Places

Now a days there are laws governing where one can smoke and where one cannot. Just as one should not smoked in a public area, it is also impolite to sit in a smoking section and raise an objection to it.

— If you do smoke:

— Do not smoke in someone else's houses before taking permission and always use an ashtray and stub the cigarette out completely.
— Never strike a match towards some one.
— Do not litter public areas
— It is permissible to politely request a person a blow the smoke the other way.
— Do not throw a lighted cigarette out of a car.
— Always carry your own cigarettes
— It is polite to light the cigarette of the person next to you, unless of course it is awkward.
— When you take out your own cigarette always offer first to the person next to you.
— Never smoke during a meal, only at the end of it.
— If you do not permit smoking in your house, it is right to politely request the person not to do so and offering and alternative place for the same, such as the balcony.

Public Displays of Affection

Love making does not belong in public. Holding hands, affectionate greetings accompanied by a kiss on the cheek, or a quick hug are perfectly acceptable in public. Passion is not.

Good Neighbourliness

The golden rule applies here again.

Be co-operative. Making too much noise and disturbing your neighbors should be avoided. It is also right to politely request hour neighbour, to reduce noise levels when things go out of control.

Respect you neighbours privacy. You should not except to be included in all their activities and entertainments, similarly you need not involve them in all of yours. When irritations occur due to what so ever reason, do not let temper fly. Talk to them and discuss things rationally. For those neighbors who impose themselves on your professional abilities or personal time, you must simply, and gently, refuse. After repeated warnings go unheeded, one may consider making an official complaint.

Always wipe your feet on the door mat when you enter someone's house. It's courteous to offer refreshments to the guests even if they are unexpected. When a new neighbour arrives do not hesitate to go and welcome them, it is also very polite to offer them a meal as they would be unprepared to cook up one themselves. Always keep your pets under control so that they do not become a source of nuisance for your neighbours. Also it is very important to respect the training and habits of someone else's pets.

Courtesies to those with Handicaps

Never stare or indicate that you are conscious that the person is different to others in any way.

— Do not be overly solicitous to handicapped people who take pride in their independence. When dealing with a deaf person or a person with impaired hearing you must speak distinctly and reasonably slow.

— Do not distort lip movements. Be patient while talking.

— Do not shout to attract the person attention if he us turning the other way. A gentle tap will do.

— Do not raise your voice if the person is wearing a hearing aid. If your are the person who is partially deaf, wear an hearing aid.

When calling or visiting

Visits to various friends and acquaintances vary from very informal drop-in visits to formal calls. A few guidelines that may be followed are:

— There is no harm in insisting that your guest use a guest

— Every host has the right to protect his/her belongings

— If your guest prefers to tuck his feet under themselves on upholstered furniture then one could request them to remove their shoes.

— As a guest , it is rude to tour through someone's house uninvited.

— It is improper for a guest to ask to be fed, unless of course it is a drink of water. Instead of asking for a guest whether he would like to drink ask him what he would like to drink.

— No one, with the exception of closest friends and immediate family, should ever be an unexpected visitor.

— Never have the T.V. on when you have guests visiting

Meal Manners

— Unless specifically invited it is best to leave children and pets at home. When visiting a sick person, comply with the hospital rules and pay a visit at a hospitable hour.

— Don't bring gift foods that he may not be permitted to have

— Don't overstay and do not say anything that may upset the patient

— Always carry flowers when you go to visit a sick person.

— When the guests leave accompany them to their car and stay till they leave unless you live in a high rise of it is raining or too cold outside.
— Whether the meal is at home or at the white house, good manners are a part of what makes the experience enjoyable.

Posture

Ideal posture is to sit straight but not stiffly, leaning back against the chair slightly. Do not play with the table appointments. Rest you hands on your lap when not eating. You may otherwise rest your wrist on the table but not your entire forearm. It is also very well within the rules of etiquette to rest your elbow on the table and is especially true in case of women. But never do the same while eating. Do not tip your chair.

Napkin

A soon as you are seated place the napkin on your lap. At a formal dinner you wait for the hostess to dos first. Never tuck in the napkin. Never wipe you mouth with the napkin, blotting or patting the lips looks much more attractive. At the end of the meal put your napkin on the left hand side of the cover, of if the plates have been removed, then in the center. At a formal dinner wait for the hostess to do so before you do. This signifies the end of the meal.

When to Start Eating

Wait for the hostess to start before you do, unless of course there is the possibility of the food going cold till all are served. If it is a large group of people, a polite hostess will request the guest to start as soon as one or two people have been served. It is correct to reach forward to pick up something from the table, without being awkward. If it is too far, request the person next to you to please pass the item. When an accompaniment that is ordinarily served with the item is not on the table, e.g. butter with bread, it is polite to ask for some.

Serving

Be careful while doing so, so as to avoid spilling anything. Any item on a toast should be picked up along with the toast and not just the topping. This is done with the spoon under the toast and the fork supporting it. Gravy should be put on the meat or rice while the accompaniment, pickle or jelly at the side. When the host if filling up plates and passing them around to the guests, first serve all the guests on the right side with the plates being passed on to the farthest end first. Then the plates are passed on to the left side. The host serves himself last.

If you are offered a dish that you are allergic to, or have a strong dislike for then it is proper to refuse very politely. The old rule that one should never leave anything on the plate is outdated, but never take a large portion and leave it untouched. Decline a dish by saying "No thank you".

The Silver

You always start with the cutlery that is laid at the outer most part of the cover. You move from outside to inside as each course concludes. The only exception is when the table has been layed incorrectly. When you have finished with main course the knife and the fork are placed next to each other n the dinner plate diagonally from the upper left to the lower right. The handles extend slightly over the edge of the plate. If the dessert is served in a deep bowl or a stemmed bowl then the spoon is placed on the plate beneath it. If a shallow bowl has been used, then it is proper to leave the spoon in the bowl itself.

Using the knife and the fork: The right way to use the knife and the fork is to hold the knife in he right hand and the fork in the left hand and both should be held in the "pen hold" fashion. The American style of changing the fork and the knife from hand to hand after the meat has been cut is perfectly right. But it is best and much easier not to. You eat the meat with the fork while it is still in the left hand.

Basic Etiquette of Eating

The basic etiquette of eating all foods is that they only be transported to the mouth in manageable, bite sized pieces. However, for certain courses and for certain specific foods, there is a certain amount of dexterity involved in it's handling. When presented with something you have never eaten before, such as escargot, what you do depends on the company you are in. If you are in the company of friends there is no harming asking one of them to show you how to handle it. However at a formal dinner, it is best to delay the beginning by talking a sip of the wine and seeing how the other do it.

Finger bowls

They are placed a the side of each diner's place either at the end of a "hand-on" dinner, or just before a dessert at a formal dinner. Dip your fingers one at a time and then dry you hands on the napkin.

Handling eating difficulties

Food that is too hot or spoiled—For hot food quickly take sip of any cold beverage. But, in case there is no drink available of the food is too spoiled it is all right to unobtrusively spit it out onto your hand or the fork and place it at the corner of the plate. Never use the napkin for this purpose.

Food stuck in the teeth - Tooth picks should not be used at the table, and certainly do not use your fingers. Wait till the end of the meal to dislodge it.

— Don't lean back and announce "I'm through", etc

— Don't wear an excessive amount of lipstick, it will stain

— Don't ever leave your spoon in the cup

DINING IN RESTAURANTS

Reservations

When choking on food cough it out onto a napkin and place it on the plate, or if need be for a prolonged cough, excuse yourself from the table.

Coughing, Sneezing or Blowing your noise - It is not necessary to leave the table to perform any of these. In case the bout is prolonged excuse yourself form the table. Never use the napkin for this purpose. In case you do not have a handkerchief, go to the nearest bathroom.

Stones, bugs, hair etc. in food—There is no remedy to this than to quietly remove it. If it doesn't upset you, continue with your meal, otherwise, leave the food aside without calling attention to it and embarrassing your host. But if you are in a restaurant, inform the waiter and get a replacement. Spills-in case of a spill, neatly clean it up with a clean spoon or the tip of a knife. In case of a stain, dab a little water on it with the corner of the napkin.

Some Dining Don'ts

— Don't encircle the plate with one hand while eating with the other
— Don't push back the plate after you have finished eating
— Don't put liquid in your mouth, if it's already full
— Don't wipe off the tableware in the restaurant
— Don't crook your finger when picking up your cup
— Don't wave round your fork with food in it.
— Don't cut up your entire meal before you start
— Don't pile up accompaniments on top of the meat on your fork
— Make reservations in one name only. When you call to make a reservation be sure to give in all the details about the group. Also mentions special preference if any. In case you are going to be delayed or are canceling your reservation be sure to call up and inform.

When waiting for people at a restaurant;

If you are the first to arrive at a restaurant wait for the next person to arrive before you seat yourself. Always inform the head waiter that you are expecting a person request that he do shown to the table on arrival. It is proper to order one's drinks while one is waiting. While being seated all women precede men. However a host always leads the way to the table. He should in fact prior top to everyone's arrival make sure of the seating of his guests if possible must be catered to. While paying the bill never display the total, and quietly put the money into the folder.

Ordering cocktails and wines

Ask all the guests what they would like to drink and in case any one doesn't drink always offer a soft drink. Wine should preferably be ordered after the food order has been placed. Choose a wine that goes well with food ordered. If you do not recognise the wine labels it is always proper to ask the wine waiter's suggestion on the choice of wine.

Ordering food

There is nothing wrong with sticking to the old custom of the man ordering for the woman. But in case the waiter asks a lady for her order directly, she should not insult by relaying the reply through her male escort. Always show some consideration for the host's wallet while ordering, unless you know that he is very well off. At a restaurant table never comb your hair or run your hands through your hair. At the most what a lady can do, is to powder her nose or apply a little lipstick at the end of a meal. Family and friends, even thought they are more important to us in our lives.

Young children

All youngsters should be taught from their childhood that there are certain rules that are to be obeyed. Obedience to a "no" is perhaps the earliest lesson one must learn. Fair play among children is really good sportsmanship. Teach children the practice of kindness, taking turns and sharing. Do not let them get into the habit of interrupting. Teach them courtesies like please and thank you they should also be taught how to greet people. Another important lesson to be given early is table manners.

Older children

Just they have been taught respect your privacy, learn to

respect theirs. Insists on good clean grooming, no matter what the latest fashion is. They should be taught the art of being a good host or a hostess. Teach them telephone manners and should set certain reasonable limits for them to receive and make calls.

Husbands and wives

Neither a husband nor a wife should make a social contrary to what is popularly believed, it is permissible to taste your partners food, if done unobtrusively. At the end of the meal if here is a lot of food that has been wasted there is nothing in asking the waiter to pack it up for you to take it home.

Should be treated with utmost respect and one should give them all the love and affection that they deserve. At the same time parents and in-laws should learn to respect the privacy and the decisions of their children and must no interfere in their lives.

Elevator Etiquette

Everyone at the front of a crowded elevator car should automatically get off, when the doors open, even if they are not their destination floor. The people behind cannot possibly emerge with ease if the people in front do not exit to give them enough room to move. If everyone on the car is going to get off at the same floor, then the people in front should get off smartly and to the side, again to make it easier for those following behind. Traditionally it was customary for gentlemen tô perform every kind of contortion necessary to allow ladies behind them to leave the elevator car first.

The best way to call the waiter would be to raise your hand so that you attract his attention. If you don't manage to do so you can call out softly "waiter" or you could ask a waiter standing nearby, to call your waiter. While paying a check the total should never be disclosed and the payment should be made quietly. In case there has been a mistake, get the waiter's attention top it quietly and never create a scene. When splitting the check it is best to ask for separate checks if the group is small but in case the group is large, then the person who has been acting as the spokesperson should take enough amount of money from everyone to cover the amount for the food as well as the tip.

Inter Relationships

Often we reserve our best behavior for company and often for strangers, giving less than our best to our. Engagement without consulting each other. Of all the advice one could give a bride or the groom, perhaps the best world be to use the words "we", "our". Even a husband and wife should respect each other's privacy and should not pry into each others mail.

The Interview

Walking into an interview without preparation may limit your chances of getting the job. You should follow the common courtesies involved in sitting for an interview. Listed below are a few to act as a guideline.

— Listed below are a few to act a guideline.

— Dress conservatively. Nothing should be too loud or glamorous. You must be dress for the purpose.

— Do not smoke.

— Be on time. Never keep an interview waiting. Do not sit until you are asked. Then sit in the chair indicated.

— Be neat. Make sure your shirt is tucked in, your shoes polished. No hems or cuffs should be frayed to raveling. Your hair should be combed and not falling over your face. Women should avoid excessive jewelry.

— Throughout the interview, follow the rules of common courtesy. Shake hands when you leave. Thank the interviewer for the time spent and the interest shown. Smile. Thank the interviewer's secretary on the way out.

— Don't name drop even if you know important persons speak with self-confidence. Answer the interviewer's questions fully so that you may amplify the facts of your resume with specific details. Let the interviewer lead you into subjects of discussion.

— Do not waste time on unsolicited information. Do not be afraid to ask questions.

— Do not apologies for your lack of skill. Instead, admit that you do not have it but you are a quick study and would be more than willing to learn.

— Know when to leave. Some interviewers rise indicate the termination of the interview, other wind up verbally with phrases such as "I have enjoyed talking with you". Be sensitive to this and rise promptly to take your leave.

— After the interview, write a thank you letter. Not only is this good manners, but it helps the interviews keep you in mind when another job appears.

— If you have not heard from the company two or three weeks after your interview, you may write a letter or phone the interviewer, expressing your continuing interest in the position. If you still receive no reply, let is rest. Persistent inquiries serve only to irate.

Your Arrire .

The clothing you wear and your overall apperance makes

an immediate impression on a pontential employer. An investment in one superb 'interview suit' is a worthwhile one. In addition the following points must be kept in mind regarding grooming for the interview.

— Shoes should be well heeled, clean, and shined.

— Hair should be neat.

— Jewelry should be at a minimum, tasteful, and not nosiy.

— Stocking should never have run, men socks should be long enough to cover their legs should the pants ride up when you are sitting down.

— Accessories should be practical and neat. This is not the time to have a bag or brief case bulging with unnecessary items.

— Accessories should be practical and neat. This is not the time to have a bag or brief case bulging with unnecessary items.

— Fingers nails should be scrupulously clean shaped.

In the winter, the outerwear should be clean and in very good condition. Whether a Secretary takes your coat and hangs up or you carry it over you arm into the interview, a ripped lining, dirty collar or spots do not make a good impression.

Presenting Yoursekf

The rules for a job interview are the same for an experienced manager as they are for a college graduate;

Be on time for the interview.

While waiting in the reception area:

(a) Read everything you can on the company that is available. Hopefully you have already located an annual report well ahead of this interview and know everything on it.

(b) Be friendly and nice to the receptionist. She may be an invaluable aide.

— Take several copies of your resume with you and make sure that they are neat ones.

— Don't take a seat until the interviewer motions you to sit down.

— Listen first and foremost. It is more important to know what the interviewer is saying than to articulate what you want to say.

— Know your strengths and skills, and bring them forth at the right time. There's a thin dividing line between self-confidence and braggadocio. You can kill your chances if you cross that line.

— Don't sound disappointed if the job in question is not the one you hoped it would be. Give it your best shot. It might turn out to be more interesting than the one you had heard about. If you left a company for a negative reason mention it simply as a statement of fact, and briefly but don't try to get the interviewers sympathy. Don't be a whiner; there is nothing that will turn off the other person faster than to have you complain unendingly how unfairly how have been treated.

Letters of Condolence

Intimate letters of condolence are too personal to fellow a set form. One rule, and one only, should guide you in writing such letters. Say what you truly feel. Don't dwell on the details of illness of the manner of death; don't especially to a mother who has lost her child, try to convince her that her loss is indeed a "blessing in disguise". The more nearly a note can express your sympathy, and a genuine love or appreciation for the one who ha gone, the greater comfort it brings.

Starting the Job

Work hours, lunch hour, vacations, company policy on sick and personal days. How often you are paid, what deductions are taken out, what benefits you are entitled to and how salary raises are awarded. There are also additional sets of business needs. Not only must we follow a code that smoothes personal encounters, but we must confirm to standards of behavior that make professional encounters pleasant and productive. When certain procedures may seem awkward or wasteful to as you begin work in a new situation, resist the urge to make immediate changes. Establish in your mind, other peoples priorities before asserting your own.

Every Office has its own protocol for who is called by his or her first name and who is called by the title. Listen carefully how people are addressed. If you happen to work in a 'little' office, even if you know someone who is your senior on a one to one basis, do call him by the title when other s are around. If you work in an informal office, you should still wait for the other person to invite you to use the first name before you do so.

The first day on the job, your new boss or his secretary will take you through the office, introducing you to your co-workers. Make a point of listening to their names so that you can remember their names. Unless invited to, do not go on a first name basis. In return you should suggest that they call you by your first name as well.

Shake hands as you are introduced. If you are seated, rise even if you are older, you are after all newer at the job. At lunchtime, if no one has invited you to join them, you shouldn't invite yourself, along. Instead, leave the office for a while, if just to walk around the block or have lunch outside or as the circumstances may have it. Do not sit alone at your desk feeling sorry for yourself. It will not do. Do not watch out for the clock and race out the moment the clock strikes closing time.

On the Job

The human needs that arise when groups of people meet in social situations are similar to those that arise in business-the need for respect and sensitivity to feelings

Asking for help

What ever your position in the company, there is never any need to bark orders or make a request sound like a demand. You'll receive more willing help if you pepper your requests with 'please' and 'thank you'. It is easy to forget human niceties on the job and the tone of voice can often tend to be offensive. By making request 'you' rather than 'I' statement, you are implying that your junior or colleges have a participatory place in the process. This leads to a more harmonious environment.

Appointments in Your Office

There are frequent occasions when visitors come to your office. There should be a defined code of conduct followed in order to ensure that courtesy is extended to each visitor. In case of a visitor dropping early for an appointment, your secretary should be instructed to greet them graciously hang up their coats and offer chairs. In case of visitors who are waiting long, it is essential to extend to therm more courtesy. It is a good idea to keep a stack of magazines in the lounge and organise foe service of eat or coffee while he waits.

While waiting in the office lounge, you are expected to sit quietly and not bother the employees with conversation in order to pass time. Do not display impatience with obvious glances at your watch. If you are kept waiting for over twenty minutes, you can always leave your business card and offer to come back when the person is not so pre occupied. Courtesy to the secretary, no matter how angry you are at her employer, is demanded.

Greetings

Whatever your sex, you rise when a superior or an older person whether male or female, enters. You rise for a client or a customer. In case your secretary comes in, or any of your colleagues come into your cabin, you generally do no stand, unless it is for the first, introductory time. At one time etiquette dictated that a woman always be the first to offer her hand when greeting a male business associate. This is no longer the case, both amend and women offer their hand to clients, customer's people outside the company and anyone they are meeting for the first time.

While speaking with a visitors during an appointment you should bear in mind that listening is as essential as talking. The listening should be done not only with ears but with the eyes and the body. You must speak with candor and control. Avoid raising your voice and negative statements, a even a No can be said courteously.

Nothing is more irritating than continuos phone calls interrupting during an appointment. If this seems likely instruct your secretary to hold all calls except emergencies until the termination of the appointment. Where this is not feasible, keep the calls you take short and to the point. You can always excuse yourself and get back to the person later. Many people find winding up an appointment difficult since they do not want to hurt the other feelings. If you see that the caller is veering away from the subject matter, you may shorten it by asking him to summarize the points under consideration. Or you may have the secretary come in and remind you about the next interview you have or you can inform the visitors about the same. It is very polite to rise when the visitors leave the office.

Appointments in other Offices

When taking an appointment in another office, courtesy dictates much of the visitors behavior as well as the host's. The thumb rule is to be on time. If you are going to be late, It is advisable to call up and inform the concerned party. When ushered into an executives office, introduce yourself if you have not met before. Exchange handshakes and the greetings of the time of day. Since the executive is undoubtedly busy, it behooves you to get to the point of the meeting as quickly as possible. Avoid anecdotes, jokes and references to your personal life. Most of all, be sensitive to the host's efforts to wind up the meeting.

Receiving Business Callers

Be on time. Even if you are five minutes late it is enough to start off the appointment on the wrong foot. The person you have come to see may be exceedingly busy and may not want to see you at all. Don't make demands on the secretary or receptionist while you are waiting. For example, "May I use your telephone?", "Can I borrow some stamps?", "Would be able to get a check cashed for me?" It is perfectly all right if the person you have come to see offers you assistance of this nature but do not ask for it yourself.

Whether you accomplished your mission or not during the appointment, thank your host for having received you and leave promptly when it is time. It can be a very embarrassing situation telling a colleague about his offensive body odur, bad breath, undone buttons or files etc. The decision to tell the offender is relevant to your personal If the visitor has no appointment and is just calling on you for an informal discussion, or to sell his products or services, he will be accustomed to having to wait. He should be treated with respect, however—a comfortable place to sit, something interesting to read and of course the company's annual report and other publications.

A person with an appointment needs special treatment if kept waiting at your office. Sometimes, a series of emergencies will play havoc with your schedule. If you are keeping someone waiting for more than ten minutes, take another minutes, take another minute to leave your office and go and greet your appointment and apologise for the delay. Give your visitor the option of another appointment, which in most cases he will reject, hoping you will meet your obligating to him soon. When you are finally able to receive your visitor, apologies again with sincerity explain the nature of the emergency, and then give him your undivided attention.

Making Business Visit

Don't take it out on the secretary if you are kept waiting. After a delay of fifteen minutes you certainly have he right to ask how much longer it will take, but don't keep interrupting, complaining about the delay. Always be polite and when you leave the office, say "thank you". If your host must take a telephone call while you are there, ask if he would like privacy for the call. If he says no stay, where you are, don't stare at him while he is talking (very disconcerting), and instead of absentmindedly reading the documents on his table(which looks pretty much like snooping), look every where else in the room-the pictures on the wall the view from the window, the pattern on the rug, etc.

When Co-workers Offend

It can be done very tactfully, as the person probably does not know that he has such a problem. If a person is unaware that he is committing an offense, it is better to inform him about it rather than allowing him to spend the day in an office in the situation. It would be more embarrassing and may be too late when he finds out later for himself or herself.

Situation of Gender

— Whoever gets to the door fist opens it.

— Whoever has the lighter handy should light the other's cigarette.

— Both men and women should shake hands with the others there is no protocol in the office for who offers his hand first.

— Some rather generalised suggestions may be useful. Certain rules apply to all meetings, no matter to run smoothly, effectively and on time.

— If everyone would assume equal gender status and focus on simple courtesy there would be no problem or confusion about who should do what for whom.

— Whoever is closest to the elevator door should enter or exit first. Both men and women should rise to greet a client or office guest, whether the guest is male or female.

— Which ever gender is hosting a business lunch pays for it.

— Personal chores, such as sending a secretary to do some shopping is a request and not part of the job unless specified a time of the interview.
— Neither men nor women should like terms of endearment in the office like 'honey' or sweetie.
— Even if your instinct, whether man or woman is to practice your outside- the- office manners in the office, don't. For example, a business luncheon is not a date. A woman should not except her companion to race to seat her, nor should he feel compelled to do so . She fends for herself, just as he does.

Leaving the Job

Notify your employers of your resignation as soon as you have decided on the date you will leave. You may inform your employer in person or in writing, explaining the reason for leaving, suggesting a terminal date, and expressing appreciation to your boss and to the company for the help and the opportunities you have received. After reading the, letter your boss will speak to your, at which time you may repeat orally what have written. Check if your company has regulations specifying how much notice is required. In any case, do not give any less than two weeks' notice. If you have a highly responsible job, it is better to give the company a month in which to find a replacement.

Some companies may ask you to help interview for your replacement. Do so with a positive attitude, no matter what your reason for leaving be. If you are job hunting while still employed keep it quite. Arrange for interviews for during lunch or before or after work so that they will not interfere with your job. Before leaving bid goodbye to all those with whom you have worked and indicate a wish to keep in touch.

How not to resign

— Don't tell your employer you are leaving for another job until the job is absolutely certain.

— Don't use an offer an other job as mean of manipulating your employer to give you a raise.

— Don't speak against the company you are leaving whether inside or outside.

— Don't brag about your new job to the co workers in the office. Don't let down on the job because you are leaving continue to be cooperative and hardworking.

5

LODGING INDUSTRY

Tourism is a hospitality industry providing a service to visitors in a warm and welcoming way. Tourists are people who for a variety of reasons travel to destinations, where they stay at least one night. A healthy vibrant industry is important for the national economy and job creation. Tourism makes an important contribution to employment. By its nature, tourism is a highly labour intensive activity as it relies so much on personal service. It is probably the sector of the economy, which is least vulnerable to substitution of labour by technology.

Tourism has also an important role to play in the bringing of prosperity to those underdeveloped parts of the country, which for various reasons, are relatively unsuited to industrial development or agriculture. Tourism's expressed natural effects complement Government's policies to achieve a balanced growth throughout the whole economy.

The hotel sector represents a vital part of these earnings, since the provision of accommodation, food and beverage is essential for anyone spending time away from home, whether it is for business or pleasure. As the nature of the traveler will vary, so the category of hotel available to them will differ accordingly. The star rating system is based upon the facilities, which the hotel offers, and the service they provide. This may be as basic as a room with breakfast, or as sophisticated as the service offered in a luxury five-star operation.

The decision to stay in a particular hotel may be influenced by various factors. One will certainly be the price. The guest will, however, be influenced by other variables such as the facilities on offer, or the location, or the size, or the standard of service. Many guests are loyal to a particular group or chain of hotels. They always seek out an establishment in which they feel the surroundings to be familiar.

Hospitality is treating people like you would want to be treated when you are traveling. In other words, it means making a tourist feel totally welcome as not only your guest, but also the guest of the complete family of the Hotel. Hospitality is genuine smiling face. Hospitality can be termed as deliberate, planned and sustained effort to establish and maintain mutual understanding between an organisation and public i.e. business of making and keeping friends, and promoting an atmosphere of better understanding.

Hospitality activity covers everything i.e. providing attentive and courteous services, facilities and amenities to a traveler, meeting and greeting him at the door, providing efficient and caring service of food and beverage to him in the room i.e. providing A Home away from Home; and making his visit a memorable and pleasant experience. Reception, welcome and, in general, the treatment of a guest pr a stranger in most friendly manner is Hospitality. In most of the countries all over the world a guest is received with a great amount of courtesy and warmth and is provided with entertainment.

The basic concept of Hospitality is to make the guest feel that he has come amongst friends and that "Guests are always welcome". Although the basic concept of hospitality has remained the same, yet with the passage of time and development of technology and science, the needs and wants of travelers have changed greatly thus providing numerous services and facilities in terms of accommodation, and other basic needs such as food and beverages.

In olden days kings, lords, maharajas, landlords and sometimes the panchayats etc. used to provide food and shelter to travelers and their animals free of charges and it used to be a benevolent activity. But with the passage of time it has not only remained a benevolent activity but has become a flourishing business too.

A part of hospitality activity is being attentive, alert, and cordial with the guest without forcing yourself and your ideas on to him; at the same time being very polite and cooperative. All those working in hospitality industry have one common objective— "Creating an image of friendly reception and treatment" for guests and visitors.

As front office personnel, the hotel staff, in order to provide hospitality should make his guests feel at home and use pleasant tone of voice smilingly, offers his assistance wherever possibly can be provided. Don't ignore the guest, and don't be abrupt no matter how busy you are: anticipate his needs and wants and provide the same without his asking them.

As an hotelier, keep on checking the hospitality attitude of your organisation. Make a checklist and be sure that you and your-staff are fulfilling each and every point of the checklist. The checklist may include areas such as front desk arid lobby, etc. Make sure that the front desk is always kept clean, orderly and well lighted. Even the stationery used is so designed that it does not create confusion and clearly indicates how it is to be filled in, and. is inviting.

The lobby is kept clean and furniture kept at proper place. Lighting system is soft and appealing. The welcome spirit that the guest is looking for is there. Floor covering, pictures, furnishing etc. are appealing, attractive and aesthetically designed.

Hospitality business now is both profits making as well as non-profit making. For example, commercial hotels are profit making while canteens, cafeterias and religious catering outlets such as langars and bhandaras are non-profit making. Hospitality industry provides services, which are need oriented, and the services vary with the needs. For example, the needs of a business executive shall be a business hotel while the needs of a student is generally a youth hostel. Traditional ways of providing hospitality in our country varies from place to place.

Hospitality in one of the hotels in France. Singing melodious songs at the time of departure of a guest is done in one of the resorts in Fiji. All the above-mentioned examples along with many others reflect the concept of hospitality provided by highly trained and experienced staff. Through their sincere efforts every guest feels like a VIP and a welcome syndrome is generated. The past, present and future of the hospiality industry are linked together. Comfortable and sanitary lodging was once considered the exclusive privilege of the wealthy only, but with the rise of industry and democracy, hospitality has now become available to common men also. Hospitality has both influenced and is being influenced by cultural, social and economical changes in society. Hospitality business tends to satisfy human needs and also play an important role in the satisfaction of social needs such as belongingness, longing ness, love, esteem and status.

Hospitality Market

Hospitality has a very vast market. All those who have

stayed in hotels or have plans to stay in hotels or any other lodging establishment can be put under hospitality market. Hence all travelers including tourists, visitors, businessmen, leisure travelers, pilgrims and company executive's etc—can be the hospitality market. Depending upon the purpose of travel people can be classified under either commercial hospitality market or leisure hospitality market.

Common Law states that a "Hotel is a place where all who conduct themselves properly, and who being able to pay and ready to pay for their entertainment, are received, if there be accommodation for them, and who without any stipulated engagement as to the duration of their, stay or as to the rate of compensation, are while there, supplied at a reasonable cost with their meals, lodging and other services and attention as are necessarily incident to the use as a temporary home."

A hotel may be called as an establishment where primary business is to provide to the general public lodging facilities and which may also furnish one or more of the various services such as food: beverage, laundry, uniformed services etc. Hence, hotel can also be called as home multiplied by commercial activities. The term 'Hotel' refers to 'a house of entertainment of travelers'.

The word 'Hotel' is of ancient origin, but its use in English for a house offering lodging and food for travelers is recent. The Hostlers of London took the name of Inn keeping in 1473. The world Hostler' or 'Ostler' having come to mean an inn servant.

The term 'Hotel' was used in England in about 1760. British law as a "place where a bonafide traveler can receive food and shelter, provided he is in a position to pay for and is in a fit condition to be received" defines hotel or inn. In legal terminology a: hotel is an inn and is required under common law to offer to its visitors lodging, food and protection, 10 their baggage. Hotel service is generally based on these three fundamental necessities of life. In addition to these a modem hotel provides its visitors many luxuries of modem urban city living, all under one roof.

History of Lodging

Early history of accommodation for travelers can be traced back to the Greek word 'Xenia', which not only meant hospitality but also the protection given to a traveler from discomforts. The city was bound to offer hospitality. In Sparta city, although due to rigorous customs visitors were not encouraged, yet goddess Athena was considered as protector of strangers and hence her name was 'Xenia Athena'. In this period travelers were mainly diplomats, philosophers; intellectuals arid researchers. Guests were invited to stay with noblemen.

In ancient Olympia, buildings constructed with the aim to accommodate strangers can be seen. They were called 'Leonidio' and were, built in 4th century B.C. The concept of hospitality can also be drawn back to ancient times. Homer finds mention of it in 'Iliad' and 'The Odyssey'. Hotel keeping can also be traced back to many centuries and its evolution through the, ages has been brought about by Britain's economical and industrial changes and developments.

During the seventh and eighth centuries, it was thee monasteries that applied hospitality to strangers and, as no charge was made for the accommodation, a travelers were expected to contribute according to their means to the Abeey funds. As more people began to travel they grouped themselves together not only for company but for mutual protection from highway and robbers.

Consequently travelers arrived in groups at a monastery and it was often difficult to accommodate them all. To overcome this, separate lodging houses, called 'Inns' were built. The word 'inn' came to mean a 'Lodging House' and until the passing of the Hotel proprietors Act in 1956, it was the legal term for 'Hotel' and hotel proprietors were legally referred to as 'Common innkeepers'.

'Common' in this sense referred to Common Law. In the thirteenth and fourteenth centuries, manor houses, being hospitable places; willingly gave accommodation to travelers. As no payment was expected, travelers tipped the servants as a 'thank you' for the generous hospitality received—thus the practice of tipping was born.

When high taxes crippled the generosity and hospitality of the owners of the manor houses, many became commercial inns. During Elizabeth the First's reign, posting houses were established and travelers, in addition to getting refreshment were able to change horses before continuing their journey.

The turn of the century saw an era that was called the 'Belle Epoch' when the grand and luxurious hotels flourished. A few hotels are still operating today. In London and some other cites attempts have been made to recapture some of the grandeur of the past era in the making of modem hotels, and bring back the memories the grand hotels of olden days.

The next stage in the cycle of evolution of the hotel industry was the coming of the motorcar. It enabled people to visit those parts of the country not reached by railways. This gave birth to inland resorts and the hotel Industry began to flourish. International air, travel has helped create the modem 'stop-over' hotel. With the increase in this form of travel, the number of hotels built close to airports has multiplied. Another trend in hotel keeping is the motel, which is the twentieth-century version of the old 'Coach Inn'.

People traveling the country by car, stopping overnight here and there, require not only refreshment for themselves, but also safe parking for their cars. Post Houses, developed by the Trust House Forte Group are in fact the modern version of the old coaching inns.

Development of Hotel Industry: An Indian Scenario

In India too the development of hotel industry is closely linked to travel. In India travel was mainly on animals(mule, horse and camel) and for rest during their travel at strategic points Dharmashalas, Sarais, Chaupals of Panchayats, Chowthry (in South India) and temples and religious places were provided by rich People such as Rajas, Kings, Zamindars etc.

Usually free accommodation and food for travelers was given. During medieval period it was mandatory for the state authorities to provide food and shelter to the wayside traveler. These developed during the Muslim period. Many famous and well known musafir khanas and sarais were made in the Sindh province during the Arab invasion, and also at Peshawar and Lahore. Mohammad Tughlak and Feroz Shah Tugalak made inns in the northern part of India.

Later, Sher Shah Suri, Akbar, Jahangir and Shah Jahan made inns in different parts of India. Jahanara Begum built a very beautiful sarai at Sahibabad (Begamabad) and its beautiful garden is still there and is called Queens Garden or Azad Park The fountain in the upper garden has the inscription "Gar Firdaus Bar Rui Zaminast-Haminhastu, Haminhastu, Haminastu".

Delhi has always been traditionally hospitable, and we find overwhelming evidence of this in the innumerable sarais and rest houses of this ancient city. Delhi has been built seven times in the area spanning from Mehrauli to

Shahjahanabad. Delhi is belived to be the oldest living capital of the world. During their reigns rulers of Delhi built sarais throughout their kingdom for the comforts of travelers.

The sarais afforded a baoli or a talab (a bathing tank), a stable, a dargah for prayer and sometimes a bimarkhana—a place for sick and ill travelers. A sufi or saint also lilved often in the sarai. Many rulers such as Allauddin Khilji banned the selling, consumption and drinking of spirits in sarais. Most of the sarais in Delhi belong ot the Slave Period. As per Shiab-al-din Alumrai there were 2000 Khangabs and sarais in Delhi and its suburbs. Most of these have not survived. Some of the famous sarais in Delhi are mentioned below:

— *Qutub Sarai*: At the entrance of the tomb of Kamali Jamali, it had a 50 feet deep baoli in its courtyard.

— *Ladha Sarai*: Also called as Baghi-Nazir, it is 300 yards south of the tomb of Jamali. It was built in 1748.

— *Lado Sarai*: Also in the same vicinity, it was originallyl a caravan sarai.

— *Sarban Sarai*: It is in Kamlapati Garden, very close to Delhi-Qutub Road.

— *Daud Sarai*: It is situated about 500 yards south of the tomb of Maulana Quli Khan in Qutub area.

— *Kallu Sarai*: Built during Tughlaq period, it is in the vicinity of Sarvpriya Vihar area. Its main feature, a rubble masonary building, is called as Bijay Mandal.

— *Arab ki Sarai*: It was built in 1560-61 by Hamida Banu Begam, wife of Humayun, as a settlement of 300 Arabs (whom she had brought with her while returning from a pilgrimage to Mecca)

— *Sheikh Sarai*: It was named after a popular saint Sheikh Allauddin who lived there and had his tomb during his own lifetime.

Some more popular sarais of Delhi are Sarai Shahji built in Mughal period, Gur Ki Sarai on the eastern side of Karnal Road with its mosque of Hyrewali_ Sarai Bangash near Fatehpuri mosque, Sarai Topkhana, the Dargha Shah Sabi Baksh with its musafir khana on Faiz Bazar road, fai Sarai on southeast of Hauzkhas village, Katwarig Sarai in the centre of the village, Phus ki Sarai, Ghatu_Sarai, Nepa Sarai and the famous Yusuf Sarai, etc.

Many small and big Indian hotel groups are operating in various parts of India. Apart from India, some international hotel chains such as Sheratan, Hilton, Ramada, Sofitel, Meridien, Hyatt and Mariott are either operating or planning to operate in India on franchise basis.

Welcome Group: It is the hotel division of I.T.C. Ltd. ITC entered into hotel business in 1975 with the opening of Hotel Chola Madras. The logo represents a traditional Indian welcome in the form of Namaste in an open doorway with the slogan "Nobody gives you India like we do". The motto of Welcome Group is "We enjoy people" Welcome Group has hotels in various cities) India such as Agra, Delhi, Aurangabad, Jaipur, Goa, Gwalior etc.

Oberoi Hotels: Rai Bahadfur M.S. Oberoi started his hotel career as a clerk in 1922 at Faletti's Cecil Hotel in Simla. Later Mr. Ernest Clarke sold his share to Mr M.S. Oberoi, who under the deed of dissolution dated August 14, 1934, became, the sole, absolute, and exclusive owner of Clarke's Hotel, Simla and Delhi. Mr. Oberoi later took over the Grand Hotel at Calcutta on lease and by the end of World War II, the Grand Hotel became a byword for good service and elegant comfort in hotels. He established Oberoi Hotel Pvt. Ltd. in 1946 and later, an 26th May 1949, established East India Hotel Ltd. (EIHL) at Calcutta. Many hotels were added to EIHL during the period.

Later two very important hotels were added -Oberoi Intercontinental in August 1965 in New Delhi and Oberoi Sheraton in 1973 in Bombay. EIHL is now one of the largest and one of the most reputed hotel chains of India with hotels not only in India but also abroad. Oberoi has a hotel training institute at Delhi and future plans of expansion.

Hotel Ambassador, New Delhi: 0ne of the flagship hotel belonging to Lala Ram Parshad who is considered as one of the pioneers of the Hotel Industry in India (now managed by Taj Hotel in Delhi). In 1946, he purchased two hotels in Mussoorie, UP. and operated one hotel in Bokaro. Lala Ram Parshad was appointed Technical Director of Hotel Ashok, New Delhi during its constructian stage and was the first Asian to be se1ected as an executive member of International Hotel Association, (I.H.A) in 1969. He was amongst the first few hoteliers to realise the importance of trained manpower in hotel industry and was associated with various Hotel Management Institutes and Food Craft Institute in India.

U.P. Hotels and Restaurants Ltd: Famous as Clarke's Group of Hotels, it was established on 13th February, 1961. It started with its flagship hotel Clarke Shiraz Agra. Later hotels—Clarke's Awadh, Clarke's Amer, and Clarke's Varanasi at Lucknow, Jaipur and Varanasi, respectively, were added to this chain.

Ritz Chain: A chain belonging to R.N. Kapoor family with hotels at Mumbai, Hyderabad, Kolkata and Coonoor (in South India). Specialised in Italian cuisine.

Spencers: Started hotel business in I 912 in Calcutta. Purchased Connamera Hotel in Madras and opened West End in Bangalore, Malabar at cochin and Trivandrum, Blue Mountains at Kotagiri in 1942 and Savoy in Ooty in 1943. Vegetarian hotels in Madras (Geetha, Ashoka and Ajanta) and Hotel Arakua in Banagalore.

Sinclairs: A chain of hotel operating in eastern part of the country with hotels at Darjeeling and Takadah.

Hotel Corporation of India(HCI): A corporation set up in 1971. It started with its first hotel at Bombay in 1974. Later hotels in Delhi, Srinagar, Rajgir etc. were added to this group.

International Corporate Hotels

These are large chains, which are almost household words in the industry, such as Hilton, Inter-Continental, Hyatt. Some of the groups are a combination of company owned, franchise and management contract operations while others are entirely owned by an individual or a company.

Their main features include standardisation of service, facilities and price, and many chains endeavor to operate a hotel in most major capitals throughout the world. Some countries have national hotel companies, which operate hotels at home and abroad, such as, the Taj and Oberoi hotel groups. These are both Indian companies which are well known outside India.

Not all groups of hotels are large or widely dispersed. Some companies own a group, which may consist of no more than four to five hotels, and they may be confined to a particular area such as the beach resorts. These are hotels which are privately owned or independent of any company. Many guests enjoy staying at an establishment of this type because of the individuality of the operation.

Hotel Consortium

Independently owned hotels form a liaison which provides them with the advantages of shared advertising costs, bulk purchasing and referral of bookings. The guest has the advantage of knowing each hotel in the consortium will be of similar standard and price. Best Western Hotels is an example of! worldwide network of independently owned hotels.

Development in the field of transportation, communication and increase in population had effect on the growth, type and location of hotels and supplementary accommodation. The classification of these hotels and supplementary units with in the industry is a complicated task.

Hotels are of various types depending on number of factors like the nature and facilities offered, size, location etc. Classification in the real sense separates accommodation into different categories or class on the basis of objective criteria, for example, by the type of accommodation, such as hotels, motels, tourist lodges, holiday camps etc. It seeks to present information about tourist accommodation units in a form, which enable the user to find information he requires. Information thus obtained will help to compare like with like.

Classification of Hotel and Catering Industry

The first comprehensive standard industrial classification (SIC) for the United Kingdom was issued in 1948. The classification was revised in 1958, in 1968, and in 1980. All the revision have been grouped by an interdepartmental committee representing the main government department collecting and using the statistics. The 1980 SIC groups economic activities into nine divisions each of which is then subdivided into classes, which in turn be sub divided into groups and finally into activities.

Hotel is an establishment selling service-food, drink and shelter. The value and the potentiality of a hotel is assessed by the size, location, the number of rooms and other revenues earning points it possesses. The classification of hotels with in the industry is a complicated task. Hotel can be classified on different basis. Followings are some of the basis of classification:

According to type of plan (Tariff pattern):

— American Plan (AP)
— European Plan (EP)
— Continental Plan (CP)
— Modified American Plan (MAP)
— Go-plan
— Barmuda Plan

Most of the hotels generally run on plan system. There are various types of plan, which are internationally recognised. Hoteliers according to their convenience or the policy of the management can adopt these. The list in which the prices of hotel services are incorporated is known as hotel tariff. On the basis of tariff pattern hotel are divided as follows:

European Plan

In this case only the lodging i.e. bed is offered. Thus the charges are made for lodging only. The client is free to take or not to take teas, breakfast, and meals in the hotel. He has a choice of eating at any other good restaurant. The guest is booked to pay for lodging only and is charged separately for all other things or services he enjoys or consumes.

This system is generally followed by youth hostels or hotels which are situated in metropolitan cities. European plan hotels fix the prices of rooms separately so that guest may either have their meals in the hotel dinning at its regular prices or go to the other restaurant. In India most of the hotels are being run on European Plan. Almost all the public sector hotels are run on this basis.

Continental Plan

In the case of continental plan bed and breakfast are included in the charges. Thus bed is offered along with breakfast and the client is, however, free to take his meal and tea as he likes. Thus the guest tariff includes lodging and breakfast and for other he is separately billed.

American Plan

Hotel where American plan is prevalent, board lodging is provided in the charge. The tariff fixed includes board and lodging. It is an all inclusive full board tariff. Accommodation and three meals daily are included in the price of the room. It includes bed, breakfast and two principal meals and evening tea. It does not include EMT nor coffee after lunch, or dinner. The needs are usually 'table d' hote'. It is also known as 'full pension'.

This means that guests day ends about 24 hours after his arrival that is, the guest arriving between lunch and dinner is entitled to retain his room until the next afternoon and to have dinner the first night and breakfast and lunch the following day for the fixed rate.

This analysis is mostly used at those tourist resorts, which are not situated in big cities. Most of the tourists who do not want to carry too much, has go for all inclusive accommodation so that the entire amount is paid at the starting point. These terms are supposed to be sold to the guest, though for internal record, a clear apportionment of charges between accommodation and meal is made. This is particularly important where some guests stay on inclusive terms and others not.

According to American plan only one charge is made to guests for room and board. But they separate the rate, applying part of it as room sales and part as restaurant sales. The distinction is necessary because of the two more reasons:

— If a guest has a launch at hotel both on the day of his arrival and the day of his departure an additional charge is to be made for extra lunch.
— If a guest arrives after dinner and leaves before lunch he is entitled to some credit for the two meals he did not eat, but which are included in his daily tariff.
— The rate should be divided into two-fixed sum for meal and the reminder for the room.

The American plan was started in the 1930's and 40's when "Americans were churning around the west, and the upstart cities were springing up". In 1955 the American Plan had become so standard that when the original Parker House opened,)t become known as one of the first hotel in USA to operate on the "European plan" meals and room change being made separately. The American Plan specially suited the resort where families might stay for the season and many resorts even to day operate on the American plan.

Modified American Plan (MAP)

The tourists mostly prefer this plan, as it is comparatively flexible. It is offered in most of the good hotels and is normally by arrangement. It includes hotel accommodation, breakfast and either lunch or dinner in the price of the room. Thus, in this type of accommodation bed and breakfast and along with it one principal meal, lunch or dinner, at the discretion of the client is also included. It generally includes continental breakfast and either 'table d' hotel' lunch or dinner in the room rates. It is also known as demi-pension.

It has been observed that the Indian style hote Is in India follow the European plan, and the western style hotels which cater the foreign tourists, operate the American plan. In the past foreign tourists used to visit

India for pleasure and leisure trips. They had plenty of time to travel and stay. Nowadays, we have typical tourists, businessmen or travelers, who would like to visit the country for a week and the city for a day. They do not have time and desire to return back to their hotels again and again.

There are good restaurants and nightclubs outside, which are equipped with comfortable furniture and super decor. Therefore, they like to enjoy their lunch, dinner outside. Under these circumstances the American plan once famous for its acceptance, became inconvenient for the foreigner. He is forced to come for the different services offered. It restricts the freedom of the guests. Therefore, the American plan is being discarded and most of the hoteliers and the tourists preferred the European plan. The hotels all over the world have shifted to European plan. In America; Europe, Far Eastern countries and other important tourist destinations, the American plan is out dated and outmoted.

The location of hotels and the type of guest it hopes to attract are two principal factors, which make important difference in the style of one hotel against another. The entire hotel differs in appeal and personality and according to the people who operate them and the people who patronise them.

International Hotels

There are modem western style hotels in all large cities as well as important tourist centers. These have been classified on the internationally accepted star ranging from 5 star to 1 star hotels. These are the hotels of international repute having more than 200 rooms with their counter parts in all the large cities. These establishments provide accommodations, restaurant facilities, grillrooms, banqueting suites and bars as an integral part of their businesses.

There normal activities are often 'supplemented by shops' of diverse kinds, garages, laundry and similar services. Also, in many instances, residential, furnished and unfurnished flats equally belong to the over all operating company. For example, in India Oberoi Hotel have some luxurious 2 or 3 bedroom apartments or a contemporary 4 bed room cottages. It provides swimming pool and landscaped lawns.

Executives, who by the very nature of their responsibilities are the leader of their profession, direct enterprises in the international group. A number of these hotels belong to the luxury class. Their service embraces the finest amenities procurable and a high pitch of comforts prevails throughout and charges are scaled accordingly. A few establishments offer all the amenities of a luxury hotel upon a more commercialised scale and at the popular prices.

Hotels in the international grouping are mostly owned by public companies and controlled by a Board of Directors. The President/Chairman of the Board is usually a prominent figure of the industry, the secretary, a chartered accountant, and the managing director, a leading personality in the hotel industry. The overall operational responsibility of the company's affairs falls to the managing director.

These hotels are generally divided into various departments under a resident/general manager who is, directly responsible to the managing director. The relationship and responsibilities of the departmental heads, general manager and. Managing director should be clearly defined and understood. The general manager manages the hotel through his departmental heads and all immediate operational data are his responsibility. The managing director takes charge of the broad operational and financial policies of the company.

Apart from the profitable lettable accommodation—the suites, flat lets, and studio rooms:-a considerable revenue is extracted from catering. There is a restaurant, which opens for luncheons and where also there are tea dances, and evening dinner dances. Good band and international fame cabarret artists are employed. The cliental dances to famous bands and are entertained by well-known cabaret artists.

True to tradition the restaurant specialises in entertainment, the grillroom caters for the epicures and the banqueting suites, large and small, handle. all the special and functional catering. The new thought in maximum revenue promotion from catering advocates three main regular activities over and above the banqueting business and the room service on the floors a large restaurant for entertainment operating a moderate "allin" tariff, a popular priced cafe complete with snack-bar and a small, select grillroom, a rendezvous of the gourmet working on a high price allocate service in return for the finest fare that money can purchase.

The practice of operating separate kitchens from the restaurant, grill and often functional catering, gives way to one large production unit under an executive 'chef de cusine', This considerable centralisation, which includes bringing the whole catering industry under a chief executive, follows the new policies of scientific operating which aims at streamlining production costs, greater economised working and increased efficiency. It is, of course, very dependent upon the actual layout and design, of premises, but quite definitely it is the policy of the future. The potential of the international hotel is limited. There is a need for limited hotels in a particular region. These hotels are opening able in the largest of communities where there are prosperous businessmen.

Residential Hotels

These hotels can be described as an apartment house with hotel service and for this reason are often referred to as apartment hotels. The rooms are sold on yearly or monthly leases, furnished or unfurnished, single or 'as suite'. Nearly all hotels in this category operate restaurant and render telephone, laundry and valet service. Rents are usually collected monthly in advance which charges are billed weekly. These hotels are mostly situated in big cities and operate almost exclusively under the European plan.

A purely residential hotel is not a hotel in the legal sense of the word since its tenants are not transients. Its methods of operation are quite similar to those of residential hotels. They serve a few rooms for visiting friends of their tenants, and most of them are glad to accommodate other transients in order to fill rooms that may be vacant. Example of such hotels is Oberoi Apartments, Qutab Hotel, and Oberoi Maiden etc. These are the largest group of all. They meet great need that of the resident. An endless mixture of varied sizes of residential establishments exists ranging from a few exclusive hotels to boarding houses of all kinds.

Many of the quieter residential towns, large cities abound with these establishments. This group can be classified by the wealth of their patrons. The guests are drawn from different walk of life, people of independent means, from retired folk living on investments or pensions and from-men women wage earners. The residential hotel is the development of USA, evolving after people discovered that permanent living in hotels offer many advantages. A residential hotel usually apartment building with the service of a hotel, maid and linen services, dinning room and room services with board and possibly a cocktail lounge.

Some are luxurious, and offer full suites, whereas others are moderate and feature single rooms. Although they are few in numbers, they usually let a room for a long period of time. In some of the cases their terms are weekly. They have fixed hours for breakfast lunch tea, dinner etc. These hotels are generally in the hands of private operators. Services and amenities provided are comparable to that of average well regulated home. The food is more or like a home style. As the residents are having fixed income, therefore it arises a number of economic problem for the owner.

The revenue of residential are more or less fixed where as the operating cost is increasing day by day. There are some advantages. The rent from room is fixed although most of the times these people are away from their rooms and secondly they are much less trouble some than any other residential. These types of hotels are the product individualistic family system. These hotels are found in USA. Terms are weekly. The turnover of residential is very slow, especially in good houses, although the more enterprising of residential housekeepers frequently set rooms aside for regular short stay visitors.

The general standard of comforts of establishment can be described as adequate and resembles that of the average well regulated home. There are set hours to rise, to breakfast, lunch, and dinner. Though public rooms are provided the guest spends much of their time in their bed sitting studio type rooms. These hotels are usually privately owned owner operated. The staff consists of one or more waitresses or waiters, cook, kitchen and floor maid etc. The food is more home style. The economic of residential establishment has its problems.

The average owneroperated house is purchased as an investment. If the terms are moderate and comforts are good, there should be few vacant rooms. But the question of terms, in an area of high operation costs, raises its difficulties where one considers the residents, whether retired or working, rely for the most part on fixed earned or invested incomes. The earnings or revenue of residential seldom increases but the operators' costs are never static. Operation with assured weekly rentals coming in must pre-budget their costs and set a side their profits to a good degree of exactitude. In short, scientific approaches should be applied.

Professional people and similar salaried wage earners are always sought after. They are only in for meals, are out of their rooms and off the premises most of the day and their rentals is guaranteed. Further more it is found that the working guest is usually much less trouble some than many of other types of residents. The practice of letting rooms unfurnished as well as furnished, deserves much consideration. Many people have their own furniture and like to have it around them and this has its advantages.

The future of the residential establishments relies upon the service flat Service flats range from great block to smaller houses letting out one room letting out one room flat lets. The block of flats has its own restaurant, catering for residents and chance customers alike, and operates a room catering service. Experience has shown, that with this type of restaurant unless there is a possibility of strong and regular chance trade, both luncheon dinner and functional, the venture can prove very precious. Small one room flat both furnished and unfurnished are always good propositions.

The latest thought advocates the equipping of small kitchen units comprising cooker, freezer and wash-up for those who find for themselves. Sometimes a room service is available in the form of room trays. The flats are centrally heated and serviced. Apartment houses of this nature are more reasonable to live in than guest houses, offering a fuller and more personal service. Residential premises equipped to be operated in the self-help idiom with a much labour—saving equipment as possible and the entire outfit designed to warrant the minimum of maintenance is the answer to high costs will become the guest house of the future for people of limited means.

Semi-Residential Hotels

These hotels offer its rooms at weekly or monthly rate or daily rate. The rates arc reduced for prolonged occupancy. They also attract permanent tenants who do not wish to be bound by lease, as well as many transients who want to take advantage of the reduce rate for longer stay. They also operate under the European plan and are situated in cities.

Transient Hotel

Most of the people are away from homes for a day, week or month on business or for pleasure. A transient hotel is one that caters to the need of the traveling public while they are away from home. This type of the hotel is the direct descendent of the old inn, operated primarily to accommodate the traveler. It distinguishing character is that it sells its room including board if operating under the American plan, without previous agreement with the guest as to the length of his stay.

Its rate is fixed on the per day basis. These hotels situated in large cities are operated almost exclusively under the European plan. In smaller sites some use the American plan. It is the usual custom of transient hotel to render a bill for all service at the time of the guest's departure, or if his stay is longer than a week, at the end of the seven day.

Commercial Hotels

Commercial hotels direct its appeal primarily to the individual traveler for business reasons, although some do have permanent guests. This hotel depends mainly on executives and on the individual traveling for pleasure. Thus these hotels mainly cater for the commercial traveler and they are not found in all the larger provincial towns. As the hotel caters primarily to business people, it is generally convenient to establish these hotels near to office buildings, restaurant and entertainment outlets.

All firms with connexions upon a nation wide scale send out their representatives on the road. Some 'reps', hi1ly an area to cover, others range the whole country, some travel with a display of goods, other travel light all have travel and lodging allowances. Commercial travelers, with their set and often-limited expenses require in expensive accommodation. But being for the most men from good homes, they require a certain standard of comfort. These businessmen like company and enjoy getting together with their fellow travelers. For these reasons there are commercial hotels catering for their needs. The commercial requires good, plain, home-style food, a comfortable bed, clean surroundings and a place where they may read or write in peace.

Stock rooms, let at a rental for displays, are usually available at these hotels. Facilities typically include small meeting and conference room, a medium sized restaurant and lounge and a swimming pool. Since occupancy at there hotels usually declines on weekends, many hotels have installed elaborate recreational amenities, health club, tennis court, all-year-round swimming pools. Commercial hotels are normally owner run and a successful business depends upon their operating on a friendly and comfortable use. A good name is a sound asset with the 'knights of the road', who, amongst their community will recommend the good and warn against the not so good house.

Success again depends upon the building of a consistent and regular business. The commercial is certainly a regular caller and will always patronise and remain faithful to a house where he is known and where a warm and comfortable welcome is guaranteed. The number of rooms in these hotels varies around the fifteen mark. The average guest stay is of short duration, though some have a wide area to cover and make the hotel their headquarters.

Meals are served at fixed hours, the principal ones being breakfast and dinner, luncheons not always being required. The terms are on a bed and breakfast rate with additional charges for all other meals. As many of the guests come by road there should always be nearly parking and garage facilities. Conventions are also another important source of business in many larger transient hotels. Conventions, sale meeting and exhibits not only attract many people to help fill the hotel rooms, but also utilize the hotels group business facilities—meeting room, exhibit areas and private dinning rooms, thus generating a additional revenue from the rentals of these spaces and the sale of food and beverage to these groups.

In some of the big industrial towns largely fully licensed commercial hotels exist complete with grill room, functional accommodation and garage, It must be emphasised that the commercial hotel is not and should never be taken for a poor type of lodging house. Neither should a bad concept be formed of the traveler. The modern commercial is an important businessman, a representative carefully selected by his firm. Marked attention is paid by the sales director to engage the right type—a man of education and integrity, because its representative knows a firm and obviously he must be carefully selected.

Hoteliers who make a specialisation of catering for the commercial traveler not only find a regular and remunerative business, but a pleasant task as well. The commercial is invariably loyal and appreciative, easy to get on with not a lot of trouble and regular in his patronage.

Airport Hotel

The location of airport at a long distance from city, the growth of the airline industry, the increase in air traffic and the postponement or cancellation of flights, has made the airlines companies responsible to take care of hundreds of passengers and built the hotels near the airports. The glaring example of such hotels is the Centaur Hotel at Delhi and Bombay owned by Hotel Corporation of India, a, subsidiary of Air India. Similarly there is an Airport Hotel at Calcutta owned by the ITDC.

These hotels get business from other travelers who require a place to rest while waiting for connecting flights. Many travelers prefer to arrive at the airport the night before and get a good night rest at these airport hotels. In addition to room, restaurant facilities, coffee shop and main dinning room, most hotels have added banquet and meeting rooms to attract the social functions and meetings from companies located nearby, in order to run their business profitably. In most of the big cities these hotels are favorite location for area meetings, as it result in saving in taxi fares and times.

Grading separates tourist accommodation into different categories or grades on the basis of subjective judgment or of a combination of these and objective judgments such as standard of amenities and services. The tourist need to know the availabilities of accommodation which meets his requirements as to type, price, amenities facilities and other criteria. A grading system provides qualitative judgment on the amenities and facilities of a particular accommodation unit. It enables the user to choose the quality of accommodation he is in need of. The physical facilities, food and other services of the establishment are graded individually or collectively.

Star Category Hotels

In addition to the approval of a hotel project at the planning stage from the point of view of its suitability for foreign tourists, the hotel on completion is inspected as a functioning establishment or approval and placement in the appropriate "Star" category. There are five such categories ranging from 5 star for hotels which offer luxury features, to one star for hotels which offer adequate standard of comfort and cleanliness. For the guidance of entrepreneurs in planning a hotel to qualify for a particular category, the government dearly lays down the facilities expected of establishments in each category.

There are no uniform criteria at international level for grading and classification of hotels. When inquired the reaction of the tourists, it was pointed out that it is more important to list facilities alone with the rates fixed, thereby giving them the choice to select. Quality is more important to them than the physical aspects of a hotel.

Many hoteliers pointed out that the star system creates an impression of luxury and waste—an artificial label with unwanted connotations. Material criteria's are unsatisfactory. These criteria's 30 not contain any built in guarantees. Facility wise, a luxury hotel will not merit any consideration of, for instance, it does not employ sufficient personnel. Quality of service is very important consideration. After all, hotels constitute a service industry.

The standard for gradation of hotels in India are laid down by the government of India from the points of view of the suitability of the hotel for foreign tourists. All hotels which are approved get worldwide publicity through tourist literature published by the government and distributed in India as well as abroad/overseas and are eligible for foreign exchange for their essential imports of equipment and provision and for their advertising, publicity and promotion abroad, from the government's special quota of foreign exchange for tourist promotion.

In addition to the approval of a hotel project at the planning stage from the point of view of suitability for foreign tourists, the hotel on completion is inspected 25 functioning establishment for approval and placement in the appropriate star category.

There are certain general features, facilities and services expected of establishments in each category. For example, hotels in the category of four, five star, and five star deluxe should be completely air-conditioned, three star hotels need have airconditioning in only 50% of rooms; two star hotels need not serve continental cuisine and one star hotels need have only 25 attached baths.

According to the regulatory conditions for approved hotels, the officials of the government or any other officer deputed by it to inspect hotel premises from time to time will be allowed free access with or without prior notice. In the event of breach of any of the conditions by the hotels, the government shall have the right to withdraw the approval.

Complaints regarding luggage having been rifled, valuable stolen and impolite treatment of the staff are common from the guests. In most of the hotels left the message in the guest rooms requesting them to deposit their valuables and jewellery with the management. Similarly, in some of the hotels the air-conditioned plants have not worked effectively. The guests also make many other complaints.

The government, who forwards it to the representatives of the region concern, also receives many of these complaints. These representatives find it impossible to complain and take the action against them because of their friendship with the hotel management. Not only this, these representatives are well known to the staff of the local hotels and therefore, are not in a position to carry out a surprise check of the hotel's facilities and services.

A satisfied tourist will help in the development of tourist traffic. A dissatisfied tourist will be injurious to the tourist industry and spoil the reputation of hotels and the tourist region. Official registration approval and grading requirements provide valuable guidelines in planning hotels and other accommodation, indicating the standard of space and facilities needed to satisfy a particular marketing criteria, conditions for grants of subsidies, loan facilities, agreement for subsequent management, are also generally linked to these facilities.

One Star Category Hotels

The general construction of the building of one star category hotels should be good and the locality and environs including immediate approach should be suitable. The hotel should have at least 10 lettable bedrooms of which at least 25% should have attached bathroom with a bathroom for every 4 of the remaining rooms. At least 25% of the bathrooms should have western style WCs. All bathrooms should have modern sanitation and running cold water with adequate supply of hot water, soap and toilet paper. The rooms should be properly ventilated and should have clean and comfortable beds and furniture.

There should be a reception counter with a telephone and a telephone for the use of guests and visitors. There should be a clean and moderately well equipped dining room/restaurant serving clean wholesome food, and there should be a clean, wellequipped kitchen and pantry.

There should be experienced, courteous and efficient staff in smart and clean uniforms and the senior staff coming in contact with guests should possess a. working knowledge of English Housekeeping at the hotel should be of a good standard and clean and good quality linen, blankets towels etc. should be supplied. Similarly crockery, cutlery and glassware should be of good quality.

Two Star Category Hotels

The building of two star category hotel should be well constructed and the locality and environs including the approach should be suitable for a good hotel. The hotel should have at least 10 lettable bed room of which at least 75% should have attached bath rooms with showers and a bath room for every four of the remaining rooms and should be with modern sanitation and running cold water with an adequate supply of hot water, soap and toilet paper. 25% of the rooms should be air-conditioned,and all rooms must be properly ventilated, clean and comfortable, with all the necessary items of furniture. There should be a well-furnished lounge.

There should be a reception counter with a telephone. There should be a telephone or call ball in each room and there should be a telephone on each floor unless each room has a separate telephone. There should be a well-maintained and well-equipped dining room I restaurant serving good clean wholesome food, and a clean, hygienic and wellequipped kitchen and pantry.

There should be experienced, courteous and efficient staff in smart and clean uniforms. The supervisory staff coming in contact with guests should understand English. There should be provision for laundry and dry cleaning services. Housekeeping at the hotel should be of a good standard and clean and good quality linen, blankets, towels etc. should be provided. Similarly crockery, cutlery and glassware should be of a good quality.

Three Star Category Hotels

The architectural features and general construction of the building of three star category hotels should be of a very good standard and the locality including the immediate approach and environs should be suitable for a very good hotel and there should be adequate parking facilities for cars. The hotel should have at least 20 lettable bed rooms, all with attached bath room with bath tubs and/or showers and should be modem in design and equipped with fittings of a good standard, with hot and cold running water.

At least 50 per cent of the rooms should be airconditioned (except in hill stations where there should be heating arrangements in all the bed rooms, dining rooms, restaurant and lounge) and the furniture and furnishings such as carpets, curtains etc., should be of a very good standard and design. There should be adequate number of lifts in buildings with more than two stories including the ground floor. There should be a well appointed lounge and separate ladies' and gentlemen's cloak rooms equipped with fittings of a good standard.

There should be a reception and information counter attended by qualified and experienced staff, and a bookstal1, recognised Travel agency, money changing and safe deposit facilities 01} the premises. There should be a telephone in each room (except in seasonal hotels where there should be a call bell in each room and a telephone on each floor for the use of hotel guests) and a telephone for the use of guests and visitors to the hotel. There should be a well equipped and well maintained air-conditioned dining room I restaurant and wherever permissible by law there should be a bar permit room. The kitchen, pantry and cold storage should be clean and organised for orderliness and efficiency.

The hotel should offer good quality cuisine Indian as well as continental and the food and beverage service should be of a good standard. There should be qualified, trained, experienced, efficient and courteous staff in the smart and clean uniforms and the supervisory staff coming in contact with the guests should understand English and the Senior staff should possess a good knowledge of English.

There should be provision for laundry and dry cleaning service. Housekeeping at the hotel should be of a very good standard and there should be adequate supply of linen, blankets, towels etc. of good quality. Similarly, cutlery, crockery, glassware should be of good quality. Each bedroom should be provided with a vacuum jug / thermos flask with cold, boiled drinking water. The hotel should provide orchestra and ball room facilities and should attempt to present specially choreographed Indian cabaret.

Four Star Category Hotels

The facade, architectural feature and general construction of the building of four-star category hotel should be distinctive and the locality including the immediate approach and the environs should be suitable for a hotel of this category. There should be adequate parking facilities for cars. The hotel should have at least 25 lettable bedrooms, all with attached bathrooms. At least 50% of the bathrooms must have long baths or the most modern shower chambers, with 24 hours service of hot and cold running water.

All public rooms and private rooms should be fully airconditioned (except in hill stations where there should.

be heating arrangements) and should be well furnished with carpets, curtains, furniture, fittings, etc. in good taste. It would be advisable to employ the services of professionally qualified and experienced interior designers of repute for this purpose. There should be an adequate number of efficient lifts in buildings of more than 2 storeys including the ground floor. There should be a well-appointed lobby and ladies' and gentleman's cloaks room equipped with fittings of a standard befitting a hotel of this category.

There should be a reception, cash and information counter attended by trained and experienced personnel. There should be a special room for conference/banquet purposes. There should a bookstall, recognised travel agency, money changing and safe deposit facilities and a left luggage room on the premises. There should be a telephone in each room and telephone for the use of guests and visitors and provisions for a radio or relayed music in each room.

There should be well equipped, welt furnished and well maintained dining rooms/restaurants on the premises, and wherever permissible 'by law, there should be an elegant, well-equipped bar/permit room. The kitchen pantry and cold storage' should be professionally designed to ensure efficiency of operation and should be well equipped.

The hotel should offer both international and Indian cuisine and the food and beverage service should be of the highest standards. There should be professionally qualified, highly trained, experienced, efficient and courteous staff in smart, clean uniforms, and the staff coming in contact with guests should understand English. The supervisory and senior staff should possess a good knowledge of English.

It will be desirable for some of the staff to have a knowledge of foreign languages and staff knowing at least one continental language should be rotated on duty at all times. There should be 24 hours service for reception information and Telephones. There should be provision for reliable laundry and dry cleaning services. Housekeeping at the hotel should be of the highest possible standard and there should be a plentiful supply of linen, blankets, towels etc. that should be of the highest quality available.

Similarly, the crockery, cutlery and glassware should be provided with a vacuum jug / thermos flask with ice cold, boiled drinking water except where centrally chilled purified drinking water is provided. There should be special restaurant/dining room where facilities for dancing and an orchestra are provided.

Five Star Category Hotels

The facade, architectural features and general construction of the building of five star and five star deluxe hotels should have the distinctive qualities of a luxury hotel of this category. Five star deluxe category hotels are a qualitative extension of the five star categories, while quantitatively, the basic features are as of a five star category. In a five star deluxe hotel, the comparative all around standard of service and amenities are of very superior quality and high standard.

The locality including the immediate approach and environs should be suitable for a luxury hotel this category, and there should be adequate parking space for cars. The hotel should have at least 25 lettable bedrooms, all with well appointed, attached bathrooms with long baths or the most modern shower chambers, with 24 hours service of hot and cold running water. All public rooms and private rooms should be fully air-conditioned (except in hill stations where there should be heating arrangements) and should be well appointed with superior quality carpets, curtains, furniture, fittings, etc. in good taste.

It would be advisable to employ the services of professionally and experienced interior designers of repute for this purpose. There should be an adequate number of efficient lifts in building of more than 2 storeys including the ground floor, with 24 hours service. There should be a well-designed and properly equipped swimming pool (except in hill stations). There should be a well-appointed lobby and ladies and gentleman cloakrooms equipped with fittings and furniture of highest standard. There should be a reception, cash and information counter attended by highly qualified, trained and experienced personnel, and conference facilities in the form of one each or more of conference rooms /banquet halls and private dining rooms.

There should be a bookstall, beauty parlor, barber shop, recognised travel agency, money changing and safe deposit facilities, left luggage room, florist and a shop for toilet requisites and medicines on the premises. There should be a telephone in each room and telephone for the use of guests and visitors and provision for a radio or relayed music in each room. There should be a well equipped, well furnished and well maintained dining room/ restaurant on the premises; and wherever permissible by law there should be an elegant, well equipped bar/permit room.

The kitchen pantry and cold storage should be professionally designed to ensure efficiency of operation and should be well equipped. The hotel should offer both international and Indian cuisine and the food and beverage service should be of the highest standards. There should be professionally qualified highly trained experienced, efficient and courteous staff ins mart, clean uniforms, and the staff coming in contact with guests should understand English. The supervisory and senior staff should possess a good knowledge of English.

It will be desirable for some of the staff to have a knowledge of foreign languages and staff knowing at least one continental language should be rotated on duty at all times. There should be 24 hours service for reception, information and telephones. There should be provision for reliable laundry and dry-cleaning services. Housekeeping at the hotel should be of the highest possible standard and there should be a plentiful supply of all lines, blankets, towels, etc. which should be of the highest quality available.

6

Reservation and Registration of Rooms

The main function of the reservation process is to match room requests with room availability. Prior to computerization era, the main function of the reservation process is only to determine basic room availability. That is to say, the reservation clerk can only tell the potential guest that a room is reserved for him/her. However, the reservation clerk can not tell you the type of the room, rate honored. Nowadays, with the wide use of reservation software package programmes, it is now possible to reserve a room by room type, rate, and to accommodate all the possible special requests of the guest. Therefore, the selling function shifted from the front office to the reservation department. Hence, projections of room revenues and profitability analysis became one of the basic functions of the reservation department. In parallel, reservation department and reservation agents should have sales goals to achieve which might focus on number of room nights, average room rate, and/or booked room revenue.

The reservation process includes the following steps:

a) Conduct the reservation inquiry

b) Determine room and rate availability
c) Create the reservation record
d) Confirm the reservation record
e) Maintain the reservation record
f) Produce reservation reports.

Types of Reservations

Guaranteed Reservation

Insures that the hotel will hold a room for the guest until a specific time following the guest's scheduled arrival date. On return, the guest shall guarantee his/her reservation of room unless reservation is properly canceled. In order to guarantee a reservation, guests might opt for one of the following methods:

a) Prepayment guaranteed reservation
b) Credit card guaranteed reservation
c) Advance deposit or partial payment
d) Travel agent guaranteed reservation
e) Voucher or Miscellaneous Charge Order [MCO]
f) Corporate guaranteed reservation

Non-guaranteed Reservation

Insures that the hotel agrees to hold a room for the guest until a stated reservation cancellation hour (Usually 6 p.m.) on the day of arrival.

Reservation agents shall make sure to encourage their guests to guarantee their reservations especially in the high season.

Reservation Inquiry

Guests can communicate their reservation inquiries in person, over the telephone, via mail, through facsimile, telex, e-mail. Moreover, reservation inquiries can be made through a central reservation system or an intersell agency.

While getting a reservation inquiry, the reservation agent shall obtain the following guestrelated information:

a) Guest's name, address and telephone number
b) Company or travel agency name
c) Date of arrival and departure
d) Type and number of rooms requested
e) Desired room rate
f) Number of people in the group, if applicable
g) Method of payment and/or guarantee
h) Any other special requests

Most of the above mentioned information is used to create a reservation record.

Sources of Reservations

Central Reservation Systems

The majority of lodging properties belongs to one or more central reservation systems. A central reservation system is composed of a central reservation office, member hotels connected together via communication devices, and potential guests.

Central Reservation Office [CRO] offers its services via a 24-hours toll free telephone numbers. Hotel members of the central reservation system shall provide and exchange accurate room availability data to central reservation offices. To illustrate, central reservation offices and member hotels shall communicate (on real time) any reservation transaction. This is possible, nowadays, with the sophisticated communication equipment available. These very equipment shall be provided by central reservation offices to its member hotels. Such equipment may range from Teletype, telex, facsimile machines, to personal computers, Internet connections.

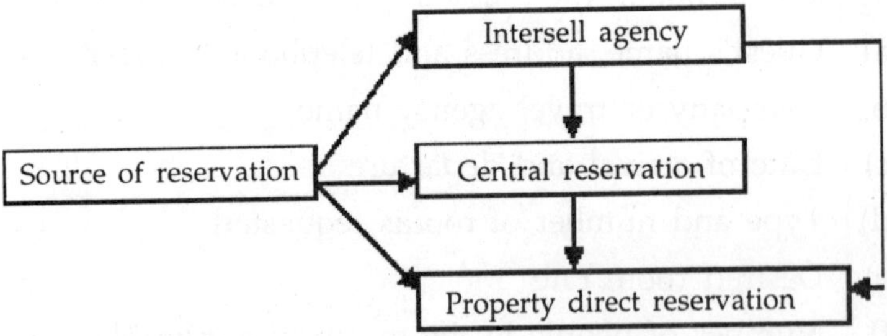

Figure 1. Sources of reservations in a hotel

On return, central reservation offices charges a fee for the utilization of its services which might take the form of a flat fee and a variable fee, or a flat percentage of potential room revenue, actual room revenue, and/or rooms division gross profit.

Central reservation offices are divided into two:

a) *Affiliate reservation network*: This very network is referred to as the hotel chain's reservation system. In fact, it is composed of a CRO, and hotels, which are members of the same chain. The main advantages of affiliate reservation network are:

   a) Streamline the process of reservation
   b) Reduce overall system costs
   c) Attract business for or refer business to another chain property

d) Affiliate reservation networks might serve, in addition to its main function, other duties like:
- Serve as an inter property communication network
- Serve as an accounting transfer tool
- Serve as a destination information center
- Serve as a connection with Global Distribution Systems [GDS]. System including several Central Reservation Offices connected to each other

b) *Non-affiliate reservation network*: A non-affiliate reservation network is composed of a central reservation office, potential guests, and member independent hotels.

Intersell Agencies

Intersell agencies are special types of central reservation offices contracting to handle reservation for more than one Product line (Eg: handle at the same time airline tickets, car rental, hotel reservation.)

Property Direct Reservation System

Even though many of the five-star hotels rely heavily on central reservation offices and intersell agencies, some potential guests might still find it convenient, and personal to call directly the hotel to communicate a reservation inquiry.

Group Reservations

Conducting a reservation request for a group shall be treated differently than accommodating a reservation of individual guests (i.e. Frequent Independent Traveler). The main reason, is that individual reservation requests are treated by the reservation department, while group reservations are initiated by the sales and marketing division, and finalized through a careful coordination of the reservation from one hand and the marketing from the other.

Below is a detailed procedure of how group reservation, in a typical hotel, is conducted:

1. A group representative, a member of the travel agency or the tour operator, not individuals, shall communicate group reservations' request to the hotel's marketing department
2. Upon availability, the hotel's reservation department shall block the requested number of rooms for this very group
3. The Hotel shall give a deadline for the group, in order to receive their final list. That deadline is called cut-off date
4. After receiving the final list, the reservation department shall change the desired number of rooms' status from blocked to booked (or reserved) rooms, and release the remaining rooms (if any left) as vacant
5. If the hotel did not receive the final list by the cut-off date, then the reservation department has all the right to cancel the group reservation and release all the initially booked rooms into vacant rooms. However, management shall use this right with precautions especially when it comes to groups reserving from travel agencies and tour operators of which the hotel is frequently operating.

Reservation Availability

After receiving a reservation request, the hotel might accept it, as it is, if there is room availability. If not, the reservation department should suggest alternative room types, dates, and/or rates, to the potential guest. If, however, the potential guest insists on his/her previous request, the hotel should suggest an alternative hotel. That's one of the main reasons why we need to maintain good relation-ships with nearby competing hotels.

The reservation department should always compare historical reservation volumes against actual arrivals. The main reason is to cope with overbooking, which a situation occurring when the total number of rooms reserved for a certain period of time exceeds the total number of rooms available for sale, for the same period of time.

In order to cope with the overbooking problem, some statistical and historical data should be stored and processed by the hotel and should be continuously updated. Such data should include:

a) Number of rooms reserved for a specific date
b) Number of rooms occupied by stayovers (for a certain specific date)
c) Forecasted no-shows percentage
d) Forecasted understays percentage
e) Forecasted overstays percentage
f) Forecasted cancellation percentage
g) Number of out of order rooms for a specific date

Equipment Tracking Room Availability

In order to function properly, the reservation department shall maintain control books, wall charts, and/or a computerized system. Whatsoever system chosen, the reservation department shall maintain and update that system to include any reservation transaction (i.e. whether a reservation, cancellation, modification). Below is a description of the three commonly used sets of equipment to track room availability under the manual, semi-automated and fullyautomated systems:

Control Books

Control books are standard three-ring, loose-leaf binders with a tally Page assigned to each day of the year. Under this very system, when a potential guest calls to have a reservation, the reservation clerk shall check the cells corresponding to rooms. If there is an empty cell for all the length of stay of the guest then the reservation clerk mark it as X (i.e. reserved). If the guest is expected to continue staying the next day, then the reservation clerk shall mark the next day's respective room cell as O (i.e. Stayover). Lastly, the reservation clerk is encouraged to use colors while updating information or the cells on the control book.

Wall Charts

These are charts stapled on the wall depicting days of the month versus hotel rooms. Moreover, upon need and convenience, these charts might be customized to track appropriate room Numbers, rates, and codes, hence, is advantageous to control books. Moreover, in this very system, different colors are used to differentiate between different reservation transactions, types of guest reserving. Lastly, wall charts eliminates the erasures and rewriting associated with control book, hence lees errors might occur.

Computerized Systems

Computerized systems are by far the best systems that track room availability. In fact, these very systems control room availability data and automatically generate many reservation-related reports in an accurate manner.

Moreover, computerized systems can itemize room availability for future periods by open dates, closed dates, versus special event dates. Lastly, this very system can forecast room availability for any reservation horizon needed in the future. In the case of non-availability of room type, the system can further suggest alternative room types, rates, or even other nearby hotels.

Reservation Record

Each reservation department shall prepare a reservation record, which depicts the various personal and financial data of guests, for each reservation transaction. The aim is to identify guests and their occupancy needs before guest's arrival. Moreover, the hotel can personalize or customize guest services and better schedule staff accordingly

In order to create a reservation record, the following items are needed:

a) Guest name (and group name, if applicable)

b) Guest's home or billing address

c) Guest's telephone number, including area code

d) Name, address, and telephone number of guest's company, if appropriate

e) Name of and pertinent information about the person making the reservation, if not the guest

f) Number of people in the group, and perhaps ages of any children

g) Arrival date and time

h) Number of nights required or expected departure date, depending on how the system is programmed

i) Reservation type [Guaranteed versus Non-guaranteed]

j) Special requirements [i.e. infant, disabled guest, or no-smoking accommodation]

k) Additional information, if needed [i.e. late arrival, method of transportation, flight number, room preferences]

At the reservation process, reservation agents shall keep in mind that a rate quoted and confirmed must be honored. Moreover, reservation clerks should be aware of the following:

a) Supplementary charges for extra services or amenities
b) Minimum stay requirements in effect for dates requested
c) Special promotions in effect for dates requested
d) Applicable currency exchange rates, if quoting rates to an international tourist
e) Applicable room tax percentages
f) Applicable service charges or gratuities

Reservation Confirmation

The hotel should communicate guests by telephone, telex, mail, or e-mail a letter of confirmation, which confirms the important points of the reservation agreement. This very letter might be shown at the registration process in order to accelerate the pace of registration and prove that the guest has the right to have a room at the hotel.

The hotel shall send a confirmation letter to all reserved potential guests, whether their reservations are guaranteed or non-guaranteed. Below are the main points that should be communicated in a confirmation letter:

a) Name and address of the guest
b) Date and time of arrival
c) Room type and rate
d) Length of stay

e) Number of persons in a group, if any

f) Reservation type [guaranteed or not]

g) Reservation confirmation number

h) Special requests, if any.

Confirmation Numbers

Hotels shall communicate meaningful confirmation numbers to their potential guests. These numbers shall have statistical meanings, which might help the hotel in maintaining an efficient historical database. Here is an example: 32 02 G JC 63

a) 32: Guest's scheduled arrival date on Julian dates calendar.

b) 02: Group reservation. In this very system, 01 might mean Frequent Independent Traveler.

c) G: means that the reservation is guaranteed. If N is written, it means non-guaranteed.

d) JC: are the initials of the reservation agent who processed the reservation.

e) 63: Consecutive numbering of all reservation confirmation numbers issued in the current year.

Registration Activities

In the semi and fully automated systems, most of the registration activities are handled at the pre-arrival stage while in the manual system they are conducted at the arrival stage.

Registration encompasses the following major activities:

1. Creating the registration record
2. Assigning the room & rate
3. Fulfilling special requests

Pre-registration Activities

At the semi and fully automated systems, guests with reservations experience (i.e. expected arrivals) experience a more rapid check-in due to the information collected by reservation clerks during the reservation process. However, at the manual system, it is inconvenient to pre-register guests at the exception of VIP's and groups. For, VIP's, even under the manual system, need to feel different than other guests. Moreover, group reservations, even though time consuming, might create time benefits at the arrival stage. Lastly, whatsoever operating system the hotel opts for, all walk-ins shall be registered at the arrival stage of the guest cycle.

Registration Record

The registration record is a collection of important personal and financial guest information. A typical registration record includes:

a) Guest name and surname
b) Guest address and telephone number
c) Company affiliation (if applicable)
d) Expected arrival date
e) Planned departure date or length of stay
f) Required room rate
g) Required room type
h) Room number
i) Method of payment
j) Special requests
k) Signature

Guest registration information items flow to different areas and functions of the hotel as shown in the following figure:

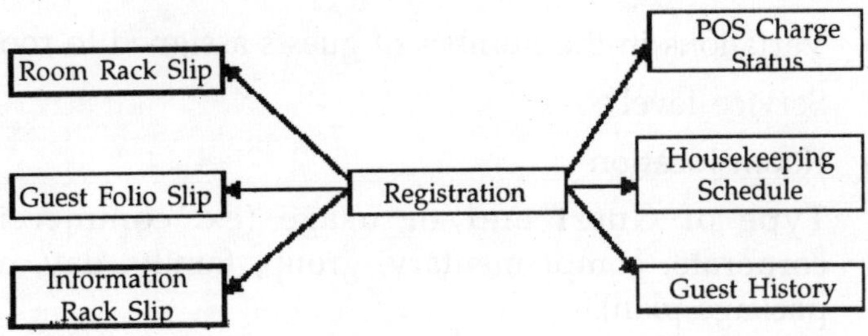

Room and Rate Assignment

The hotel shall identify and allocate an available room from a specific required room category (i.e. type & rate). That's why, under semi and fully automated systems, reservation and check-in clerks shall be sales minded while negotiating room and rate assignment with guests. This fact applies for registration clerks under the manual system. Moreover, while assigning rooms, check-in clerks shall keep an eye on hotel's future reservation commitments and not assign a room to a guest, while that very room is preassigned to some other guests at the same period of time.

Room Rates

While pricing rooms, the hotel shall keep in mind that rate should be between a minimum (determined by cost structure) and a maximum (determined by competition structure) boundary as depicted below:

Minimum (Hurdle Rate) < Room Rate < Maximum (Rack Rate)

Cost Structure < Room Rate < Competition Structure

Front office department shall finalize room rates with guests during the registration process. Moreover, rack rates shall only be applicable for walk-ins especially during the high season. Lastly, room rates might be affected by:

a) Seasonality
b) Variations in the number of guests assigned to rooms
c) Service level
d) Room location
e) Type of Guest and/or usage (ex. commercial, corporate, complementary, group, family, day, and package-plan)

Room status

At registration, check-in clerks shall contact the housekeeping department to be informed about the last status of hotel rooms so that they can assign only clean and available for sale rooms to their guests. That's why, the Front office, Housekeeping and Reservation department shall maintain a high degree of collaboration between them.

The front office and housekeeping department shall continuously update the status of each single room. Below is the typical housekeeping room status flow of any single room:

Occupied → On-change → Clean and Available for Sale

The front office and housekeeping department shall frequently reconcile and compare their updated reports (especially under the manual system) for any possible room status Discrepancy. The aim is to detect these very discrepancies before it's financially and timely too late, and correct them.

Room characteristics

In order to be sales minded and convince potential guests to accept the highest priced rooms, the front office clerk shall be aware of the characteristics of each room type, the differences within the same room category (i.e. furnishings, amenities, and location).

Room Types

The following room type definitions are common throughout the lodging industry:

— *Single:* A room assigned to one person. May have one or more beds.

— *Double:* A room assigned to two people. May have one or more beds.

— *Triple*: A room assigned to three people. May have two or more beds.

— *Studio:* A room with a studio bed-a couch, which can be converted into a bed. May also have an additional bed.

— *Quad:* A room assigned to four people. May have two or more beds.

— *Queen:* A room with a queen-size bed. May be occupied by one or more people.

— *King:* A room with a king-size bed. May be occupied by one or more people.

— *Twin:* A room with two twin beds. May be occupied by one or more people.

— *Double-double*: A room with two double (or perhaps queen) beds. May be occupied by one or more persons.

— *Mini-suite or Junior suite*: A single room with a bed and a sitting area. Sometimes the sleeping area is in a bedroom separate from the parlor or living room.

— *Suite:* A parlor or living room connected to one or more beds.

- *Connecting rooms:* Rooms with individual entrance doors from the outside and a connecting door between. Guests can move between rooms without going through the hallway.
- *Adjoining rooms:* Rooms with a common wall but no connecting door.
- *Adjacent rooms:* Rooms close to each other, perhaps across the hall.

Method of Payment

Guests, at the registration stage, shall communicate or confirm their intended method of payment. Below are the common methods of payments accepted by hotels:

Cash

Guests intending to settle their accounts by cash shall have no in-house charge privileges and, hence, all their purchases should be paid in advance (i.e. PIA status), which means that as guests purchase any kind of service or product, they shall pay for it immediately. In accordance to cash payment, registration clerks shall prepare lists of PIA guests and communicate them to all Point of Sales outlets. On the other hand, paying immediately might not suit some guests (even though intending to settle their accounts by cash), that's why hotels might give guest charge privileges, at the condition they provide an imprint of a valid card or an approved direct billing privilege at registration.

While handling cash payments, all cashiers shall be aware of counter-feats and short cash change situations! Moreover, cashiers shall be trained as to accept so many cash equivalent tools that are legally accepted as cash payment such as cashier checks, traveler checks, money orders.

Personal Checks

Nowadays, very few hotels still accept personal checks as a method of payment due to the high probability of fraud associated with this method. In fact, in order to accept personal checks, most hotels necessitates that these very checks be supported by a credit card with a check-cashing guarantee, that the amount to be cashed against checks shall be within the hotel's established limit, and preferably accept personal checks only during standard business hours where banks are open. If personal checks are to be accepted, front office personnel shall imprint the credit card on the backside of the guest personal check and record the Guest ID card or driving license certificate along with the guest's address and telephone number on the face of the check.

Credit Cards

Credit cards, nowadays, become a preferable method of payment for guests and hotels.

In accordance to this very method of payment, front office clerks should check the following items before accepting the credit card as a method of payment:

a) Expiration date
b) *Invalid credit card*: This can be checked either by on-line authorization systems, or comparing the card across some cancellation bulletins
c) Credit card floor limit

Direct Billing

Some guests (especially VIP) do not prefer to wait at checkout queues like other guests before departure. They, rather, prefer, only to sign their guest folios, go to their homes, later receive a certain invoice detailing their charges while they were staying at the hotel to be settled by payment to hotel bank accounts. In order to satisfy the needs of this category of guests, hotels created the direct billing process.

To be eligible for a direct billing privilege, guests shall at pre-arrival stage or maximum at the arrival stage fill a hotel credit application form along with the provision of an imprint of a valid credit card. This very form is sent to the Front Office manager, or Rooms Division manager for approval. If not approved, guests are requested to pay with any of the other methods of payments.

Special Programmes

Special programmes are any form of vouchers, coupons, or any special incentive awards received from businesses, airline companies.

Issuing Room Keys

With the issuing of room keys, the rooming process gets to an end. However, concerning room keys, front office clerks shall respect hotel's written policies governing guestroom key control. As an illustration, front desk agents shall only handle the room key to the guest without announcing and/or spelling out the room number. This is a vital requirement to protect and ensure guest safety and privacy. After guest is handed his/her room key, front office clerks shall offer bellboy assistance.

Fulfilling Special Requests

The front office department shall watch for any guest special requests and try promptly to satisfy them. This way creates a good and professional relationship with the guests and increases the probability that the hotel will receive these guests for another time in the future (i.e. repeat guests).

Guests' requests are usually grouped under the following categories:

a) Room type
b) Bed type
c) View
d) Location
e) Amenities

Creative Options

Some of the following innovations are nowadays commonly used while registering a guest:

a) Eliminating the front desk structure (i.e. deskless environment)
b) Having a hotel greeter register guests at a special lobby location
c) Creating a unique & separate registration area for VIP guests
d) Simplification of room process for corporate gatherings, tour , and convention groups Self registration (i.e. self check-in terminals)

7

SECURITY MANAGEMENT

Security has always been a concern for hotels worldwide. The recent increase in terrorist acts has had its toll on travel and tourism worldwide. Whilst there is no indication that hotels are a primary target for the perpetration of terrorist acts, hoteliers must ensure that their properties are secure—if anything to give a sense of security to guests and staff whilst at the same time protecting their investment.

TYPES OF SECURITY

With regards to hotels the security can be classified under following three aspects:

1. Physical aspects
2. Security of persons(guest and staff)
3. Security of systems

The Physical aspect security can further be divided into two parts:

a) Internal Security
   - Against theft(close circuit camera and burglars' alarms).

— Fire security(smoke detectors, fire alarm, water sprinklers, fire extinguishers).

— Proper lighting of corridors, fire escape, basement and other areas).

— Safeguarding assets (proper inventory, regular physical checks, e tc.)

— Keeping track of unwanted guests.

b) External Security

— Proper lighting of boundary and outside of the building.

— Proper fencing of the building.

— Fencing of pool area to avoid accidents in night.

— Planting of shrubbery can also help in restricting perimeter access of properly.

— Avoid poisonous and thorny bushes and barbed wire.

— Manning of service gates to restrict entry.

— Fixing of closed circuit T.V. cameras.

Security aspects of persons can further be subdivided into two parts:

a) Staff: A fourteen points effective programme for this is suggested as follows:

— *Effective recruitment and selection*: References checked, properly screened etc.

— *Identification of staff*: Issue identity badges and use distinct uniform for easy identification.

— *Key control*: Maid should carry the key in her possession and issuance and return should be properly recorded.

— *Red tag system*: Proper system for hotel property being taken out.

- *Training*: Proper training to employees to note unusual things, safety drills.
- *Adherence to management policy of security*: An employee disregarding policy should not be confirmed.
- *Trash handling*: Trash should be checked to see if employees are smuggling out things out of hotel with trash.
- *Employees' parking*: Proper checking of employees' vehicles at the time of going off duty. If possible it should be away from the main parking.
- *Locker inspection*: From time to time surprise checking of staff lockers.
- *Inventory records of linen, stores and other items.*
- *Bring in experts (snoops)*: Hire an outsider, bring him as an employee to check and report about the culprit staffs.
- *Security consciousness*: Guest should be told to be careful about his property.
- *Enlist employees*: Employees should be asked to report about suspected persons - guests with scanty baggage etc.
- *Set example*: Management should follow these rules and should encourage employees to follow the same.

b) Guests

- A guest suspected of taking away hotel property should be charged on the bill. Not many guests will protest if told they are being charged for souvenirs.
- Rooms should not be opened for guests coming and saying that they have left their keys inside unless their identity is established.

Security aspect of systems in hotel is equally important to physical and persons' security.

— Record all losses and missing items immediately.
— Inventory control should be proper.
— Auditing should be done on regular basis.
— Proper system for cash receipts and disbursements should be made.

The term 'systems' mean the operations of the hotel e.g. all the equipment used for operation, procedures laid down for operations and policies to be followed. The objective of such security is to safeguard the assets of the hotel. Systems, procedures and the policies followed properly shall safeguard the assets and shall increase the life span of equipment as well as avoid any breakdown maintenance. This would mean the following:

— Fix duties and assign responsibility: Fix duties of the staff so that people do their duties and don't interfere with others' work. This will help in pinpointing responsibility in case of theft, losses due to negligence and any other similar eventuality. Make people responsible for what they are doing and for equipment they are handling.
— Make surprise checks.
— Bonding of employees: People who have access to liquid assets should be bonded so that in case of any theft etc. the concerned person may be caught.
— Hiring of an independent agency for checking of your systems of security.

Room Break-Ins Security

The most common security problems are in guest rooms (mostly with the traditional, metal locking systems). Next comes the parking area. By using the electronic card key system we can reduce Room Break-Ins cases. Sometime even the traditional cards keys themselves are easy to copy. It is important to keep pace with technology and the management should have foresight while choosing a system that is compatible with future trends of technology or enhancement. Appoint a systems manager to provide the 'band aid' support to your systems. The supervision staff would be trained to change their supervisory techniques and vision. Proper training to staff should be given before installing the system. The hotel can reduce electricity consumption through the key card operated energy saving system, which could distinguish between a guest and a maid.

Bomb Threat Security

Set up security nets with bags and body searches for guests who are not known to the staff. Banqueting suites should be security checked and locked after use; it way all nonpublic areas should be treated. All cluttered items should be removed as they interfere in security checks. Freestanding deep ashtrays are suspicious objects. Toilets should be checked. Staff entrances should be secured at night. Goods received and bags should be checked and kept tidy. If we get a scare or an alert we should not ask people to evacuate the building as we could be sending them into a danger area.

Warn them to stay away from windows and leave them slightly open. Heavy curtains should be closed. If a bomb threat is received the telephonist must note carefully what exactly is said, what time the call is received, the sex, and accent of the caller and background noise if any. After the alert the G.M. should stay put in lobby where he can be reached immediately. The duties and responsibilities of staff during such emergencies should be defined. Work closely with police to keep updated on sensitive events in the area.

Bring in sniffer dogs before a big conference commences. Chambermaids and housekeeper should be trained to keep security checks in room; particularly if they notice that the carpet has been moved, they must report immediately. Just asking a guest "Can I help you?" makes people aware that we are vigilant. Fire officers should be called in weekly to check firefighting system. A drill in fire fighting and first aid should be given to all staff members. Practice in building evacuation is done twice a year.

Following are some of the safety and security measures:

1. Use of resident card (identity card).
2. Key control system should be employed. Bellboy errand card.
3. Maintain record of master key used by staff.
4. Housekeeper's occupancy report to me bade regularly, proper procedure of checking keys in rack should be followed.
5. Double lock system, magic eye and a door chain system to be used.
6. Proper "left luggage system" to be followed.
7. Safety lockers for guest valuables should be provided.
8. Modern and efficient fir fighting systems should be used.
9. Smoke detectors to be installed.
10. Proper regular maintenance of equipment, appliances and building should be done.
11. Close circuit camera at parking and other strategic areas in the hotel.
12. Fire escape route must be designed.
13. Frequent patrolling by the security staff must be made.

14. Security frisking (body check) if needed (without offending the guest).
15. Heavy drapes to be drawn during night on windows and exposed glass panels.
16. Computer and data processing security (safeguarding of computer information, so that it does not reach the competitors and protection against virus in the programme.)
17. Avoid use of hotel name and room number on keys (use code words on the fobs). Preferably use of computerised room keys or magnetic keys.
18. Employ a house detective.

Security of Women Travellers

Security is a concern for all hotel guests, but women travelers can especially appreciate certain features, such as:

— Mirrored walls of the guest room floor elevators so that you can see who is walking behind you.

— Well-lit public area such as lobby bars.

— Key cards for guest room doors instead of metal door keys that could be duplicated.

— Valet parking to eliminate the need to enter a parking garage by women.

— If a woman traveler is not assigned a guest room on the special executive floor, hotels often will, upon request, upgrade her accommodations to that floor without and increase in room rate. This floor is staffed almost 24 hours a day with a concierge.

— If possible, hotels will honor requests for rooms close to the elevator.

Fire Safety Systems

Fires in hotels are too often and may result in the injury/ and loss of life or both of the guests and staff. It also causes loss of property and tarnishing of the image of the establishment. Following are some popular system used for fire safety.

1. *Tata Honey Well System*: It is a system, which allows only the authorised personnel to gain access to a specified area. In this system each person is given an access card. At the entry point the card is given to the card reader and the information goes to the controller where it is verified against pre-programmed information and only after verification the access is granted with the help of an electronically activated locking/unlocking device.
2. Globe Alarm Electronic Fire Alarm System

Fire alarm accessories

a) Ionisation Smoke Detector: This is a dual chamber detector with American 241 radioactive material. Offers a high standard of performance and quickly responds to visible and invisible combustible particles generated by fire in its incipient stage.

b) Photo-electric Smoke Detector: This optical detector operates on light scattering principle, quickly responds to the smoke particles of fire and transmits the valid signal to the C&I equipment.

The receptionist can do a great deal to minimise the risk of accidents. The genuine accident is really very rare; most result from oversight or carelessness. It will never be possible to eliminate accidents completely but if the receptionist takes accident prevention seriously and is aware of the possible hazards then she may help to make her organisation a safer place to work. Frayed carpets, torn or badly worn linoleum, projecting nails, loose floorboards and highly polished floors—all bring about falls.

Any danger spots such as these should be noted by the receptionist and reported to the management. Visitors are always unaware of potential hazards such as an unexpected step up or down, swing doors that fly open violently and steep stairs. When a lift is installed in the building visitors should always violently and steep stairs. When a lift is installed in the building visitors always is escorted to the required floor by a messenger or by the receptionist herself.

Deliveries of stationery and office requisites should not be left lying around the reception area to trap the visitor. These should be stacked neatly out of the way until a messenger or porter arrives to remove them. The porter or messenger should not be allowed to carry awkward or extremely heavy parcels as this in itself may bring about an accident. The receptionist should always use a safe stepladder to reach high shelves.

Heavy books, box files and ledgers that are balanced precariously on a shelf may fall at the slightest vibration so they need to be stored very securely. When filing cabinets are overloaded in the top drawers, or when more than one drawer is opened at a time, they may topple forward with very nasty consequences. A great many mishaps are caused by 'bumping' into someone.

Personnel become absorbed in a report or some important papers while walking across the reception area. They may push open glass doors without looking to see if someone is on the other side and person struck by a glass door could suffer serious facial injuries. There is not really very much a receptionist can do here except to draw attention to such a situation by displaying a warning notice or special warning posters.

The staff should provide plenty of ashtrays and pleasantly request all visitors to use them if they smoke. cigarettes left smouldering on the edges of tables or window - sills are a fire hazard. The staff should not empty ash trays into a waste paper basket without ensuring that all cigarettes are thoroughly extinguished and wastepaper baskets should not be placed too near to an electric fire or other heating appliance. All personnel should know fire precautions.

The receptionist and other staff should be aware of the positions of all the fire extinguishers an should know the drill for evacuating the premises in case of fire. The staff must also know how to prevent the rapid spread of the fire by closing windows and doors and unplugging all the electrical appliances. He should, personally, escort visitors to safety if possible. In a hotel, however, it would not be possible for the receptionist to make himself responsible for the visitors. The current fire precautions, however, ensure that fire escapes are provided and fire doors installed.

Electrical cables, switches and plugs must be carefully maintained and not left to fall into disrepair. Plugs must be earthed and no sockets should be overloaded, electric machines such as duplicators should have a 'fail-safe' switch and electric fires must be guarded. The Socket should be switched off and the plug removed when equipment is not in use.

The receptionist may contribute tremendously to make the organisation to safer place to work by own vigilance and by warning the management of potential danger spots. It is the duty of the employer to consult representatives of the employees with a view to enable him and his employees to co-operate effectively in promoting and developing the health and safety at work of the employees and in making sure that the measures are effective.

Every employee has a duty while at work:

1. to take reasonable care for the health and safety of himself - and of other persons who may be affected by his acts or omissions at work.
2. as regards any duty or requirement imposed by his employer or any other person or under any of the relevant statutory provisions to cooperate with him so far as is necessary to enable that duty or requirement to be performed or complied with.

In other words, it is the employer's duty to provide and maintain a safe environment in which employees may work. It is the duty of the employees to take reasonable safety precautions and to co-operate with the management in making the organisation's premises a safer and healthier place to work.

Threats to Privacy

It is the duty of front office to protect the privacy of its guests-even and perhaps especially if they are in the public eye. It is very tempting to tell one's friends all about a well-know person who might be staying at your hotel, but you will have no control over the information passed over from your friends to their own friends. In no time at all, your guest may be pestered by fans, autograph hunters, paparazzi and reporters. However, it is not only the privacy of well-known guests that must be respected.

Every one of our guests is entitled to his or her own privacy and steps must be taken to ensure that information about our guests is not divulged to outsiders. Giving room numbers to individuals other than the persons being accommodated in those rooms is unethical and should be avoided at all costs. There is a tendency amongst representatives locally to divulge room numbers to taxi drivers, restaurants etc. It may prove difficult to ascertain whether the breach of confidentiality is the responsibility of the hotel or not, but guests have every right to hold the hotelier accountable.

Threats to Guests' Property

The hotelier's liability is limited, it is in the interests of the hotel to ensure the safety of its guests and their property - if anything to protect the reputation of the hotel. If the hotel is in an unsafe area, or in an area roamed by unscrupulous characters, guests should be made aware of this -especially if they intend to venture out of the hotel at night. In India, hotels should be especially aware of the problems caused by prostitution.

Prostitution is not per se illegal but a hotel would be acting illegally if it were to knowingly encourage or allow prostitution within its premises. It is not for us to make a general characterisation of prostitutes, but some prostitutes may well be thieves and since hotel guests will often negate their involvement with a prostitute they may accuse hotel staff of pilfering their property rather than admit to the fact that they hosted a girl in their room.

Unfortunately, we must also face the fact that there are instances where guests are robbed by staff. There may be a "social divide" between staff and guests, which may lead the former to pilfer money or valuable items from a guest (although this is by no means the only reason why guests may be robbed by staff). If the hotel has a policy of randomly checking staff's property before they leave the hotel, this may act as a deterrent and waive the hotel's liability should this arise.

Confidence tricksters or conmen may also find themselves into a hotel. There is very little a hotel can do if a confidence trickster makes his way into a guest's "life". These type of people often settle their own room accounts and are simply guests from a hotel point of view. However, when the identity of a conman is known the hotel is ethically bound to blacklist him and refuse him accommodation in the hotel. Guests themselves may also threaten each other's enjoyment.

If a traveller turns up in a drunken state asking for a room a hotel is entitled to refuse him on the grounds that he is not a fit state to be received. This is true even if he already has a booking, as he has broken one of the implied conditions of the contract. Similarly if the guest misbehaves throughout his stay the hotel is not obliged to let him stay. When guests complain about being kept awake by a noisy couple or a drunkard next door, it is not good enough to tell a guest that "nothing can be done about that." One must employ considerable tact in dealing with such situations.

Protecting Staff

Staff should be able to work in a harmonious and secure environment. In this sense, all measures taken to protect guests will provide further security for employees. Some guests are unscrupulous and although it is highly unlikely that guests will rob staff property some guests may put into question the integrity of the staff. Unfortunately this may happen to female staff who refuse sexual advances from guests. It is in the interest of the hotel to protect its staff by ensuring that the integrity of employees is safeguarded and it would be unwise for a manager to immediately accept the guest's complaint without hearing the employee's version of events.

Skippers or Runners

There a number of guests who leave without paying. These guests can generally be divided into three groups:

1. The 'accidentals': These are guests who simply forget to pay, often their extras bills. Most of these guests do not intend to leave the hotel without paying - they

simply believe their account is being settled by someone else. When contacted these guests pay their bill immediately and are highly embarrassed. The hotel should deal with them courteously.

2. *'Opportunists'*: These guests check in with the intention of paying their bill on departure, but when they realise that they can get away with not paying their bill (or simply a transaction that should have found itself on their bill - eg. last minute breakfast or minibar consumption) they make a run for it!
3. *'Premeditators'*: These are guests who, from the start, have the intention of leaving the hotel without paying. Some of these guests go into considerable lengths in order to avoid paying. These guests generally stay for short periods and will move to other hotels as soon as payment is demanded.

When hotels network between themselves they are in a position to warn each other of such guests. Experienced room staff can often detect premeditated walkouts because generally they do not unpack their belongings to facilitate a quick run. If the hotel staff communicate effectively it may be possible for a hotel to operate like an intelligencegathering machine, with the doubtful guest being reported on all his activities whilst the security manager determines whether or not he or she is a bona fide guest.

IMMORALITY

An immoral contract, under the law, is void. This will mean that if you knowingly allow a guest to take a room with the purpose of using it for prostitution, you will not be able to enforce the contract because it based on an illicit purpose. A contract must be based on a lawful consideration (Section 966 of the Civil Code)—if it is not, then it may not be enforced in a court of law. It is in the interest of a hotel to discourage prostitution, not only because it has a reputation to protect but also because prostitution may bring about a number of difficulties. Similarly a hotel must ensure that other illegal practices, such as illegal gambling, are not conducted on its premsises.

Accident Book

An accident book should be kept in every organisation and the receptionist should record all details of accident, which have occurred to employees whilst they were engaged in carrying out their normal daily duties. The book must be kept at such place as to be readily accessible at all reasonable times to any injured employee and any person bona fide.

Particulars of an accident may be entered herein either by the injured person himself or by someone acting on his behalf. The accident book when filled up should be preserved for a period of three years after the date of the last entry. Every employer is required to take reasonable steps to investigate the circumstances of every accident recorded herein and, if there appears to him to be any discrepancy between the circumstances found by him and the entry made, he is required to record the circumstances so found.

Security and Safety Booklet

Hotels usually use a folder to instruct the guest about security and safety instructions. This folder generally consists of (i) Key to security and safety, (ii) Instruction in case of fire, and (iii) Escape plan.

Security Programmes

A lodging property's management must evaluate whether

a special security presence is warranted by its property's security requirements. If it is, management must decide how that presence may best be integrated with the operation of the hotel A management team's commitment to the concept of security as a vital function within its hotel is necessary to integrate security into the day-to-day operation and administration of the property.

Setting up such as integrated security system is a process that involves many elements. These may include establishing working relationships with local law enforcement agencies, choosing whether to use in-house or contract security personnel, and creating an appropriate and effective security training programme for all personnel.

Importance of law Enforcement Liaison

Because the communities in which they are located affect hotels, a property's management may gain insight into potential security problems by looking at the crime rate and past experiences of the property and surrounding community. Liaisons with police authorities and neighboring lodging properties can help management gain an understanding of the nature and extent of local crime problems. Review with local law enforcement agencies the crime experience, trends, and current problems of your property's locale.

Developing such liaisons often results in clear benefits. In some residential communities, local organisations have developed community crime watch programmes in their areas; such programmes attempt to remote neighborhood or block activities to develop an awareness of suspicious persons or actions. Some lodging properties have adopted a similar concept that involves developing a telephone network that notifies both police and participating lodging properties when a crime has happened.

Each property notified, in turn, may call other properties in the network. Some properties find that such a programme may aid the security efforts of the participating lodging establishments. However, such a programme should be cleared with local counsel to ensure that the information disseminated does not violate Federal Trade commission regulations or other federal or local laws, or result in a suit for defamation or libel. Public safety is, of course, the specific responsibility of law enforcement agencies.

In conjunction with a property's security programme, its management should cultivate cooperative liaison with the local b ranch of these agencies. Inform them of your concern and interest in the security of your property, your guests, and ad your employees. Invite the appropriate law enforcement personnel to visit your property so they can become familiar with it. Some hotels hire off - duty police personnel as additional security staff on special occasions. If possible, review security procedures with the local authorities. Be sure to request police guidance in crime prevention and always document such efforts. A good relationship with local law enforcement agencies can often encourage a prompt response to security incidents and will probable result in your property benefiting from more frequent police patrols.

Police presence can also be a deterrent to certain crimes; measurable reductions in total crimes have been noted in some cases in which liaison relationships have been developed. Good relationships may also be very helpful and much appreciated following a security incident or during an emergency. Frequently, community police budget limitations within a jurisdiction do not permit an evaluation of crime as it relates to a specific hotel. Where a crime unit does exist within a law enforcement agency, a full review of community and lodging industry crime experience may be available.

Unfortunately, law enforcement agencies and private security personnel have not always cooperated well with each other. Police have sometimes viewed private security efforts as staffed with poorly trained older (or retired) personnel who are largely ineffective and even fairly apathetic. In today's changing security scene, this stereotype often does an injustice to a lodging property's security personnel as private security has become more professional and sophisticated. Better communication is the key to educating local law enforcement agencies about the broad scope of a lodging property's security programme and about the growing professionalism of the industry's security personnel.

The most effective cooperation results when both the police and the property understand the needs of the other. The police should know enough about a property and its security programme to be able to offer appropriate assistance in a given situation. They should be informed of any special events or visitors (for example, political or entertainment figures) that may involve an unusual security risk at the property. On the other hand, the property' staff should have a basic understanding of police procedures so that they can be of greatest assistance to the police once they arrive.

Local law enforcement authorities will be able to explain the type of assistance they would find most helpful. This information should be included in a property's ongoing security training programme. In one positive development, some police departments have gone so far as to assign a number of detectives to work directly with hotel security directors. These detectives can teach a property's personnel about police procedures and needs, offer guidance to the staff about what to watch for, and share information about any crime patterns in the area that may affect the property. At the same time, they learn about the property and its security system, improving the likelihood of effective police response in times of need.

Security Staffing

A hotel must choose whether to hire staff as full-time personnel, to contract with a local security company, to arrange for part-time protection with local off-duty police personnel, or to use any combination of these or other options. Because of a facility's size and organisational structure, it may be appropriate to assign security responsibility to a member of the management staff, such as a resident or assistant manager, a chief engineer, or the human resources director. Larger hotels have full-time security staffs, with one or more employees on each shift.

Smaller properties may not be able to afford a full-time hotel employees may be an appropriate approach. If management decides the property needs a security department, it must determine whether the department should be a proprietary unit with in - house staff functions or a security programme run through a reputable, licensed contract security company. In some situations, it may be feasible to employ off-duty police to cover certain hours of operation while e property's staff provides daytime coverage as one of their responsibilities.

If the security department or function is integrated into the property, additional considerations include determining whether the staff will wear uniforms, whether certain or all members of the security staff will be armed, and whether there are shifts on which security personnel need not be assigned. All decisions concerning security deserve careful thought and should be discussed with legal counsel. Each option has its adherents.

Contract Security: The proponents of contract security organisations argue that such organisations can provide sophisticated services at considerable savings. In addition, they assert that a reputable contract Security Company will provide thoroughly screened, tested, and trained personnel. It may also provide consulting services, including in-depth surveys of hotel security requirements, electronic audio countermeasure sweeps (a debugging tactic), data processing security, and assistance in contingency planning for bomb threats and natural disasters. Finally, they contend that an in-house security staff may become too familiar and friendly with the other employees.

If a guard catches a friend stealing, he or she might hesitate to report that friend. Some people believe that this situation may be less likely to occur if the security personnel are supplied by an n outside agency. In selecting a security company, make sure that extensive guard training geared specifically to each facility, is provided. Review contract and insurance requirements (i.e., named insured clauses and requirements for proof of insurance) with legal counsel. Check the previous lodging experience of the company management and line security staff, as well as specific training in dealing with guests, employees and others.

If your state or community requires such agencies to be certified, verify that the agency you choose meets this legal requirement. Be clear and specific regarding the services to be provided by the contract organisation. Require the security firm to conduct frequent unannounced inspections, day and night, by supervisory personnel to ensure that its guards re in compliance with company regulations. Determine whether the security service can provide a sufficient number of personnel on short notice in the case of a large-scale emergency. Insist that security officers be required to file daily and unusual incident reports.

Determine the percentage of the security firm's hotel customers retained on an annual basis; rates of retention are an excellent indication of a company's service level. When hotel management gives orders or instructions to the contract employee, a different relationship is established. The responsibility for the actions of the contract security office becomes blurred, and there are instances in which the contract employee has been considered as a workers' compensation case for the property rather than for the contract security company.

Contract companies have held and prevailed that the instructions from the hotel executive may have placed the contract employee in jeopardy and may have been contributory to workers' compensation incident. In other instances, the contract employee has turned to his or her company for the workers' compensation only. A contract security organisation will almost always be willing to perform an indepth security survey for a property if the property has not already performed one for itself or had one performed by another agency.

Remember, however, that a contract security organisation is selling services. This fact may sometimes lead such as organisation to overstate a property's security needs, which can pose unfortunate problems for an innkeeper. Suppose a property implements some)(Perhaps even most) of a contract security organisation's recommendations, yet despite such efforts, a security incident occurs on the premises. It is possible that a plaintiff might subpoena and use the security organisations written recommendation in court as evidence of the innkeeper's knowledge of alleged "inadequate security." Even if the recommendation overstated the needs, if the innkeeper failed to implement every suggestion, a jury may be more likely to judge the innkeeper negligent.

In-House Security: Proponents of proprietary or in-house security departments point out a number of advantages to this system. They emphasize the fact that the hotel has greater control over security officers or staff members without intermediate outside supervision. They also argue that training for in-house security staff members can be much more directly related to the lodging industry. They believe that those within the industry than more effectively address the peculiarities and special needs of the industry by those in a contractual relationship with the industry.

In addition, they emphasize that the quality of personnel is under the direct control of the hotel in a proprietary system, rather than under the control of the contract security company, and that the director and staff of an in-house department are more effectively integrated with the other departments and personnel of the property. If the security staff is in-house, then the security director can be a member of the property's executive committee, an action that would not be possible with a contract staff and supervision. They point out that a greater sense of loyalty may be developed among an in-house staff since career paths can be established that move security personnel into other roles in the organisation. Finally, another important concern is the constant turnover of contract security employees.

Off-Duty Police: Some properties use off-duty police officers for their security staff. There are certain benefits associated with this practice. Such officers have superior training in reacting to and dealing with crimes and other emergencies, they understand the law, they are used to dealing with people, they may be better able to identify known criminals, they are immediately recognised as authorities, and they often do in fact have more authority than ordinary citizens (as a deputised individual, they are not limited to a "citizen's arrest"). In addition, police liaison and response may be enhanced.

However, there may be potential drawbacks as well. First, police officers may be oriented more toward apprehension functions than toward prevention. Second, some jurisdictions require off-duty officers to be armed and this may not be desirable (if they are armed and injure somebody, the property may be liable). In addition, off-duty officers may not be permitted to wear uniforms in some jurisdictions. Finally, an officer may be working at the hotel following a full-duty police shift and may be fatigued.

Personnel Practices: Security concerns should be addressed during the selection and hiring of all employees. It is especially important, though, when hiring a member of the security department, given that this individual is responsible for the protection of persons and assets on the property. If legal counsel approves, the hotel could use and an authorisation statement and affidavit. Such a statement, signed by the job applicant, allows the property to more easily investigate the applicant's background.

Bonding (insuring for protection from employee theft) through an insurance company permits more effective screening of applicants and is certainly warranted in the case of security staff members who, by virtue of their function, have access to most areas of the hotel. It is appropriate to have everyone employed as a vehicle driver to have a police background check for traffic violations. This background check should be done before hiring and at least annually from that time on. This procedure applies not only to specialised employees, such as airport buss drivers, but for other employees who may drive a hotel vehicle as part of their other assigned duties, such as a maintenance staff member. Properties must also decide how they will schedule security staff on the property.

During daytime operation, involving all employees as the "eyes and ears" of the property may make it possible to reduce the security staff to a few key persons able to respond to a security-related call from an employee. In setting schedules, special programmes and activities that may affect the number of security staff needed during a particular work shift should be taken into consideration. In many properties, additional security staff members are assigned during the nighttime hours.

Customer Care

Good personal service is about creating a sense of well being in our customers-a feeling that their needs are being met, that their business is valued, that they matter to us. It is difficult to define the personal service concept as it cannot be weighed or measured. Good service will mean different things to different people and the challenge for people working in the hotel and tourism industry is to anticipate and meet as far as possible the needs of all our customers. There are two main types of service - material and personal. The term "material service" relates to the quality, quantity, price and timing of food, drink, physical comfort, information and working methods.

Material service is generally something concrete and visible that the customer can easily identify. It would not be possible to provide good personal service without the back up of good material service. Yet often the customer is unmoved by the material service no matter how good a standard it is, and it often has, at best, only a neutral effect on him. Customers are more likely to comment on material service when it is below standard than to praise it.

Because material service is easier to define and analyse, most companies give priority to this in terms of investment and advertising aspects of their business. Yet research shows that it is the level of personal service that is most often the deciding factor in customers' choice and that where the material service falls below par, it may well be forgiven if the customer is treated with warmth and kindness. Personal service is about creating a sense of well being in our customers—making them feel welcome and valued while at the same time ensuring that their needs are looked after.

Personal service is not tangible therefore it is difficult to measure, as it is largely more emotional that rational and is very subjective. While you may not be able to actually see personal service, you will notice if it is not there. The key to success in the hotel business is to provide a high standard of both material and personal service - every hotel supplies its guests with food, drink and accommodation but if your hotel is also providing a high level of personal service then you will have the competitive edge. That is the reason you and the job you do are so important to the business - you are the key -to providing a high level of personal service.

There are three parties involved in customer care and they are:

1. the customer
2. the company
3. you

All three parties can feel the benefits of good and effective customer care—there is something in it for everyone and not just the customer. These benefits may be identified as follows:

— For the Customer

— pleasant experience

— attractive, welcoming surroundings

— helpful, interested staff

— finding what they want
— being cared for and treated as an individual
— respect and recognition

For the Company

— satisfied customers
— customer loyalty and goodwill
— increased sales and profit
— good "word of mouth" publicity
— staying ahead of the competition
— meeting customers' needs for better service
— repeat business as satisfied customers will return again and again
— greater job satisfaction for staff

For You

— customers being pleasant to you
— the pleasure of seeing the customer satisfied
— the satisfaction of doing a good job and using your skills and knowledge
— knowing you have done your best
— the satisfaction of being pleasant to people and giving them what they want
— more happiness, less stress

Don't confuse the idea of offering a perfect service with the idea of having the perfect product. It is possible to deliver a really good service to guests in a hotel or guest house that has no star rating and it is also possible to deliver a poor quality service in a five star hotel! You are the central and key element in the delivery of quality - you are in the driving seat—you have a very important role to play. Providing a quality service means:

— offering a high quality experience to every customer every time
— maintain with high standards and repeat them every time
— developing systems and making them work every time
— developing routines for tasks that have to be done again and again so that completing them becomes a habit and nothing gets left out.

Even when things go wrong you can still offer the customer a quality service by sorting out the problem promptly, efficiently and courteously.

Completing Different Needs of Customer

Working in the hotel business means coming in contact with a wide cross-section of the public. In your job you will have to learn to recognise. Who your different types of customers are and the service that they will both expect and require - meeting their different needs to the highest possible standard is customer-care in action. Some of the obvious ones are:

The business and conference customers: They will expect and demand an efficient professional service to act as a backup to their activities. Their priorities might be punctuality, availability of high standard secretarial services, privacy and unobtrusive service.

The holidaymaker or tourist: They may be more interested in the hotels leisure facilities, friendly service and value for money.

It is your job to identify these individual needs and to ensure the service you provide matches if not exceeds the guest's expectations. The less obvious type of customer is those who may have special needs, requiring understanding and sensitive handling, such as:

— The elderly
— Children
— Disabled customers
— Visitors from different cultural backgrounds.

The elderly

Older customers may have mobility problems and may tire easily. Some people in their eighties are very active, others are not. Your common sense should tell you if they need special help. Elderly visitors should be treated with respect and patience.

Children

Families comprise a major segment of the holiday market, yet many staff appear to tolerate children under sufferance. Parents and children will appreciate staff who facilitate and welcome families. For instance, involving children in the commentary when accompanying guests to their room - "We have a lovely pool for children in the commentary when accompanying guests to their room" - "We have a lovely pool for children and lots of toys in our playroom", offering to heat a baby's bottle, assisting parents carry small children and so on.....these are the extra bits of service that you and your hotel will be remembered for.

With children, it is possible that they may drift away from their parents and get lost in the hotel. This can be a very frightening experience for them, try to reassure lost children while following the hotel procedures for dealing with this situation.

Disabled visitors

Disabled visitors can easily be handicapped not by their disability but by staff attitudes towards them. Try to treat them as you would any other visitor, while making allowances for their disability. Guests with restricted hearing may not be able to benefit from your announcements. During a conversation, they may be trying to lip read so it is important that you face them and speak very clearly. If necessary write down the information for that you face them and speak very clearly. If necessary write down the information for them. Similarly blind or partially sighted people may require special assistance.

Overseas visitors

It helps to understand and respect some of the basic cultural differences between various nationalities so as to avoid offending visitors unwillingly. For instance, recognising religious dietary restrictions and codes of behaviour will help you in your understanding of guests needs. Caring, being professionally concerned and noticing things is one of the secrets of success in the hospitality industry. If you care about others, you take trouble to see that they are comfortable and have everything they need. Caring is both the way you do things and the reason why you do them.

COMPLAINT HANDLING

People on holiday, traveling on business or celebrating a special occasion have high expectations of everything going well. When something does go wrong, they will often confront the first staff member they can find. The complaint will often be unrelated to you personally or to your job, but they will still expect you to solve the problem. Knowing how to respond to a complaint and how to resolve the problem will be of great importance to you in your job as a receptionist.

In many ways you should consider a genuine complaint as an opportunity and turn it around to your advantage. Remember, customers don't always complain when they have reason to. Unspoken dissatisfaction is the most damaging to any business, whereas a complaint allows you the opportunity to remedy the situation and to regain the customer's goodwill.

Most complaints are genuine and should be regarded as a very important source of information about the quality of your service or product. While many complaints are received in hotels about efficiency and the product itself, a high proportion concern staff and the way they treat customers. Therefore proper handling of a complaint can make a very favorable impression.

Feelings of anger and upset can cause customers to react differently as they complain. Some appear aggressive and loud, others are timid and there are others who calmly insist on their rights. Staffs have to cope with the moods as well as the facts of the complaint. Showing empathy - that you appreciate how the customer feels - will make things easier. It is important to avoid arguing with customers who complain - they are already angry and upset.

It is important to avoid justifying or making excuses from your own or the company's viewpoint - customers are not interested in excuses, they want results. While all complaints are different and will need a different approach, the following listen techniques in six steps offers a guideline for dealing with them.

1. *Lend an ear to the customer's problems*: The first thing he wants to do is get it off his chest. Pay concerned attention to his story. If he is really angry, let him blow his top. Avoid interrupting and never show annoyance, resentment or fear.
2. *Identify the important points*: While you are listening, sort out the important facts of the situation. Keep an open mind. If necessary, ask clarifying questions,

without appearing to crossexamine the customer or doubt his judgment.

3. *Sympathise*: "I'm sorry", is the least that can be said in the circumstances. Show that you are concerned and regret the problem or the inconvenience caused. But don't keep on apologising or be too willing to admit your hotel is at fault.
4. *Thank the customer*: Thank the customer for bringing the matter to your attention and show that the trouble he is taking in making the complaint is appreciated by you.
5. *Explain what can be done*: Make sure the customer understands what you and the company can and will do about the complaint.
6. *Now act quickly*: Whatever is to be done by yourself or anyone else, ensure that it is done quickly and efficiently.

Always try and put yourself in the customer's shoes when dealing with a complaint. Ask yourself how you would like to be treated in the same circumstances.

Follow Up

The front office staffs are responsible for the follow up procedures on a problem. This can be done either later the same day, or the following day. The staff member who dealt with the initial complaint should contact the guest and ensure that the problem has been rectified to his satisfaction.

Customers' Rights

Customers have rights, the most basic of which is the right to expect good service. They also have other rights, which have a basis in law. You should always familiarise yourself with the hotel policy as they will reflect the relevant laws in your country.

Handling Difficult Customers

All customers are important, no matter what the reason is that makes them demanding. You will find that most customers are reasonable - however you need to be able to deal with the unreasonable. Turn the difficult customer's strength against them. The following tips may help to you, should you find yourself faced with a "difficult" customer:

Type	Technique
Argumentative	Do not argue back
Disbelieving	Keep to the facts, not opinions
Expert	Give the facts and let the customer express his views
Indecisive	Show range of alternatives
Nervous	Establish confidence, do not rush
Pompous	Allow customers to maintain dignity
Short-tempered	Tact, patience and firm response
Silent	Use questioning technique

Complaint Recording

You should know the policy and procedures in your hotel for both handling and reporting complaints. If you remember, complaints should be regarded as an opportunity - not just an opportunity to make amends to the guest but also to get to the source of the problem to ensure it does not happen again. It is therefore essential that the relevant information is filtered back to the appropriate person or department so as the hotel can safeguard against the same problem occurring again and again. You should record all complaints according to the hotel policy and make sure your supervisor knows about it. The best way to deal with a complaint is to prevent it from occurring.

Both compliments and complaints are a comment from customers on the service, which they have received and are also an opportunity, to improve service. Compliments, which are passed on to staff, are a useful means of increasing motivation and of raising standards throughout the business. Praise for a job well done is always very satisfying so accept compliments from customers graciously and be sure that they are passed on to staff members concerned and that your manager or supervisor is made aware of the positive feedback. Keeping a record of special compliments and displaying thank-you letters and complimentary guest comment cards can give staff a welcome morale boost.

Do's and Dont's

Keep this list with you as a reminder of the things you should and should not do when handling complaints.

Do's:

- Listen to the complaint as if it were your own
- Identify the important points
- Sympathise
- Thank the customer for bringing the matter to your attention
- Explain what can be done
- Now act quickly and follow up

Don't:

- Ignore the problem and hope it goes away
- Ignore the guest

— Forget you have a supervisor to refer to
— Be afraid to tackle the problem
— Delay – act right away

Steps for Solving Guests Problem

Problem solving calls for systematic handling and application of innate and acquired skills. There are four basic steps to handle such problematic situations:

— Listen to the problem.
— Understand the problem.
— Find solutions to the problem.
— Follow-up on the solution.

On analysing these four steps, one realises the need for all the security personnel, to be able to listen, empathize and reason. This is because, it is their responsibility to deal with and solve difficult problems. It is important, that they don't view problem solving as a problem in itself. All security personnel should have stress and event management skills so that they are able to solve problems effectively.

The first step of problem solving, i.e. listening, should be a spontaneous reaction. This skill, if not inherently present should be cultivated. Listening is essential to understand the gravity of the problem a guest is facing. It leads to better analysis and quick resolution. Following are the guidelines that can help in honing the listening skills: One should be very attentive while listening to the guest. This can be achieved by maintaining constant eye contact and making a note of the complaints made by the guest. It is very important that one doesn't continue or conduct any activity which might convey that the personnel is distracted or is not interested. While a conversation is going on, especially when the guest is complaining, wait for your turn to speak. Do not interrupt a guest when he is talking to you. Let him finish explaining his problem first.

Accept the complaint in a positive manner, do not react in anger to a guest who is already in a complaining mood. Anger is a negative emotion and must be avoided as it is known to restrict listening and the assimilation of the conversation. It is important to take the onus of the problem. Apologize for the existing situation the guest is in and assure him of corrective measures. Under no circumstances should you evade solving a problem, by shifting the onus to someone else or passing the buck. This may only lead to an argument, which is a clear indication of the inefficiency of the security personnel in handling the guest and the problem.

Secondly, does it matter who created the problem? Desist from ducking the problem or acting as if it is a normal occurrence and hence not a problem at all. Refrain from blaming colleagues or seniors for the problem. Shifting blame reflects poorly on the organisation. One should understand that good communication always comes from good listening. Good listening reflects sincerity and concern for the guest. Sincerity in tone strengthens his belief in your ability to solve his problem. At any given time convey positive body language. This affirms your sincerity and earnestness in solving the problem and this, in turn, converts a guests' negative attitude towards your organisation, into a positive one.

The second step to problem solving is to understand the problem. This is done by defining the problem on hand. What is a problem? A problem is a situation, which occurs when the actual state of affairs differs from the desired state of affairs. For example, a guest staying with the property desires absolute safety and security standards being adopted by the hotel, for himself and his belongings. It may so happen that he complains about his laptop being stolen from the seminar he was attending at the banquet hall. Now, that is a problem and it arises only when a guest is in a situation wherein he feels threatened, or when he is faced with an event that may cause damage or loss to his person or his belongings. Unless otherwise necessitated, most problems are never referred to local law enforcing authorities. The reason could be personal and varied from the guest's point of view.

When the problem is grievous, like a guest found dead in the room or smuggled goods, drugs in the room, in such cases the management is known to consent to reference of the matter, to the police. Even in such situations, the security personnel cannot be absolved of the lack in their initial spadework.

As 'circumstances cannot lie, witnesses can and do', hence it is very important to visit the scene of the problem, example, if a guest is found dead in his room, a visit and check of his room could help determine the consequences and motive of the incident and one can establish the cause, that is, whether the cause of the death is natural or unnatural. If it is an unnatural death, the cause can be further narrowed down. Every security officer should be able to determine what physical clues at the scene of the problem will provide him with scientific evidence. It should be remembered that most physical evidence becomes useless if inefficiently handled.

Customer Care and Etiquettes

The first time you meet some one presents an opportunity that will never come your way again the chance to make a good first impression. "Hello" is the universal form of greeting and it is acceptable in any situation except after a very formal introduction. Even comparative strangers say "hello" in passing and it is the friendly response to first name introduction.

Even more informal is "Hi"; a friendly greeting for people who already know one another which should not be used in answer to a formal introduction. A verbal greeting should be accompanied by direct eye contact which indicates that you are actually paying attention to the person you are acknowledging. Verbal greetings may be accompanied by a handshake, especially during as introduction or when two acquaintances meet one another in passing.

A nod and a smile are all that are necessary when casual acquaintances pass by chance. It is safer to nod to someone whose face is familiar than to run the risk of seeming to ignore an acquaintance. Often what is perceived, as rudeness is absentmindedness. Absorbed in their own thoughts, people do not hear the voice or see the motions made by someone trying to greet them. It is important to make allowances for absent mindedness or poor eyesight before believing that you have actually been snubbed. In places of worship, or during a performance in a theatre, people should only no and smile. It is thoughtless to engage in conversation until the service or performance is over.

Talking Leave

Very often it is difficult to know how to extricate yourself from a conversation when you must leave. The most cordial way is to say, "I am so glad to have got this chance to see you but I have got to go or else I will be late for my next appointment." It taking leave of group of strangers - whether you have been introduced or not - you nod and smile a good bye to those who happen to be looking at you, but you don't attempt to attract the attention of those who are not aware that you are leaving.

Rules of Introduction

Introductions are required on many occasions; and especially when two strangers meet in the company of a mutual friend. It is inexcusably rude of the one who knows the other two to chat with one and leave the other unacknowledged and left out-standing by as if they did not exist. Te three basic rules are

a) A man is always introduced to a woman.

b) A young person is always introduced to an older person.

c) A less important person is always introduced to a more important person.

To help introductions develop into a few minutes of cordial conversation, the one making the introduction can provide additional information for the two persons. Introductions were viewed as the vital step in establishing a proper communication channel between two individuals.

Use of first names

In addition to the rule that younger people do not address significantly older people by their first name unless asked by the older person to do so, there are other persons for whom first names may not be used except by specific request:

— A superior in one's business, unless it is requested to do so.

— Person of higher rank (a governor, a diplomat, for example)

— Professional persons offering you their services, such as doctors and lawyers, who are not personal friends. In turn, these professionals should not use your first name unless you request them to.

A handshake can create a feeling of immediate friendliness or of instant irritation between two strangers. No one likes a "Boneless" hand that feels like one is grasping an empty glove, nor does one appreciate a vice like grasp that cuts rings into one's flesh and temporarily paralyses every finger. The proper handshake is brief, but there should be firmness and warmth in the clasp. It should always be accompanied by a direct look into the eyes of the person whose hand one is grasping. When a men is introduced to woman it is in her place to offer her hand or not, as she chooses, but if he were to extend his hand she must give him hers as nothing could be ruder than ignore spontaneous friendliness.

When you meet someone whose right arm or hand is missing or is deformed, extend your right hand even though he or she cannot shake hands in the normal way. The handicapped person will appreciate that you made no unnatural gesture to accommodate his or her disability. He or she will respond by offering his or her left hand, or by saying, "Please forgive me if I don't shake hands, but I am glad to meet you."

8

MANAGING HUMAN RESOURCES

HIRING

Hiring is making all necessary arrangements to prepare the recruit and current employees for a successful working relationship including processing personnel records.

Job Offers

In order to finalise a job offer, the front office department needs to rely on human resource division or someone specifically designated by top management. Front office job offers encompass into three steps:

— *Extending the offer*: In order to extend the job offer, careful wording and timing are very important. Moreover, the job offer might be in written whenever possible.

— *Negotiating the offer*: In order to negotiate the job offer, the hotel must have familiarity with applicants' backgrounds and expectations. Moreover, the hotel shall negotiate job offers only if the job offer is reasonably certain to be accepted.

— *Completing the job offer*: While completing the job offer, the hotel needs to inform the recruit that he/she is not expected to know all aspects of the job. Lastly, hotel shall start the immediate preparation for recruit's arrival.

Processing Personnel Records

— By processing personnel records, the hotel helps prepare the new recruit for his/her new position. Moreover, the way of processing personnel records shall be warm, caring, and professional.
— Apart from processing personnel records, hotels shall fit uniforms for recruits and order nametags. Moreover, the recruit should be informed about management expectations, the front office and hotel goals and policies. Lastly, the hotel needs to discuss with the recruit time cards, pay procedures, house rules, reporting instructions, and uniform policies.

ORIENTING

With orientation, a hotel ensures that the Recruit will have a Good Start at Work. During the orientation process, the following items shall be covered:

— The hotel
— The benefits
— The working conditions
— The job
— The front office team
— The hotel's rules and regulations
— The Building

Moreover, the recruit shall be handed the employee manual or handbook. Meanwhile, the hotel must complete all tax withholding, insurance. In addition, the hotel must provide recruits lockers and uniforms (if applicable). Lastly, let the recruit have an accompanied tour in the entire facility in order to be familiar with all hotel's revenue centers, and to introduce him/her to key managers.

Training

The front office manager shall ensure that department recruits receive proper training. In order to determine training needs, front office manager shall consult only job descriptions. Below is a description of how job descriptions are developed:

Job Break-downs

Job lists and job breakdowns are used to build effective skills training programme and to tailor an efficient system for evaluating performances. A job list lists tasks that must be performed, and simply state what the employee must do while performing the job (shall not be detailed). On the other hand, job breakdowns specify how each task on a job list can be performed (shall be observable, and measurable) and serve as a training guide, and as a method of performance evaluation.

Developing Job Breakdowns

In order to develop job breakdowns, the front office manager needs to write and analyse the performance standards for each task on a front office job list. The front desk staff members, who are actually or had performed the tasks before, create job breakdowns. These Members are refereed to as standards group, who shall write performance standards for at least 2 or 3 positions. Later, individual members should write job breakdowns for the remaining front office tasks. Then, all job breakdowns must be communicated to the front office manager for approval.

If they are not approved, the process shall be repeated from the beginning. If the job breakdowns are approved, final copies shall be sent to all group members or contributors for a careful analysis of job breakdowns and for simplification of procedures. Lastly, the standards group shall reach a consensus for each front office position. These finalised job breakdowns can, now, be used for training and evaluation purposes.

Training Standards

In order to train recruits to standards, trainers pass by the following four stages:

Prepare to train:

— Write training objectives
— Develop lesson plans
— Decide on training methods
— Select training location
— Assemble training materials/equipment
— Set up the work station

Conduct the training:

— Prepare the employee
— Begin the training session
— Demonstrate procedures
— Avoid jargon
— Take adequate time
— Repeat the sequence

Coach trial performances: By coaching trial performances, the trainer helps the employee gain the skills and confidence necessary to perform the job. In accordance, the trainer should complement the employee on tasks performed correctly and correct any performance problems observed.

Moreover, the trainer, after certain number of demonstrations, shall reverse roles with the trainee.

Follow through: In this very stage, the trainer shall continue positive reinforcement, provide feedback to the trainee, and continuously evaluate the trainee's progress. While doing so, the trainer shall coach only few tasks each day.

STAFF SCHEDULING

While scheduling their staff, the front office manager shall try to balance the needs of the property with the needs of their employees. To illustrate, the front office manager shall schedule students applying for part-time positions in shifts that do not conflict with their school classes.

Whatsoever scheduling the front office manager opts for, he/she shall, in most of the cases, base employee scheduling on seniority concerns. That is to say, place the more senior employees in better preferable shifts. Moreover, the front office manager might opt for one or more of the following alternative scheduling techniques to cope with seasonality, lack of labor in certain rush hours:

— Part time scheduling

— Flextime scheduling

— Compressed scheduling

— Job sharing

RECRUITING

It is the process by which qualified applicants are sought and screened to fill up open or vacant positions. This very process starts with job vacancy advertisement, which should be geared first to hotel's current employees and announced through proper sources. Later, after screening job applicants, the front office department shall move to interview and evaluate applicants in order to determine the best person for the job.

During recruiting, the human resource manager and the front office manager should communicate and cooperate with each other. For, the front office manager should identify the skills and qualities needed for a certain front office position, and then communicate them to the human resource manager. Lastly, all screened applicants shall enter to a general interview conducted by the human resource manager. On the other hand, if the vacant position concerns a managerial level, candidates shall also be interviewed a second time by the front office manager. While recruiting, front office manager can seek applicants from the following two sources:

Internal Recruiting

Internal recruiting means finding applicants from within the company. Moreover, internal recruiting is usually a synonym of transfer or promotion.

Advantages of internal recruiting:

— Candidates are familiar with the hotel and have shown proved high skills

— Current Employees, when promoted, tend to have a higher productivity and morale

— Hotel employees think that there are always opportunities for them to advance

The biggest disadvantage of internal recruiting, is that eventually employees occupying higher managerial levels tend to think, behave, act and decide in similar ways therefore, reducing degree of innovation and creativity especially when it comes to solving unexpected and unstructured problems. Internal recruiting might be ensured through the following methods:

Cross training: Cross training occurs when employees are trained to perform duties of more than one job. Moreover, there are a lot of advantages of cross training such as:

— Diversifies employee skills

— Makes employees think they are valuable to the hotel

— Permits employees to have wider range of promotion possibilities

— The front office manager can develop comprehensive department schedule (i.e. better plan employee vacations and absences due to scheduling flexibility)

Succession planning: In this very kind of internal recruitment, the front office manager identifies a key position and targets a particular employee to eventually fill that position.

External Recruiting

External recruiting means trying to fill vacant positions with outside applicants. The advantages of external recruiting are:

— Applicants tend to have more innovative ideas

— Applicants tend to have unique perspectives

— Applicants tend to possess creative ways of doing things

Similar to internal recruiting, there are several techniques to find eligible outside applicants. Some of these methods are:

Networking: Networking constitutes all the personal contacts with friends, acquaintances, business associates, educators, school counselors and/or trade members or community associations

Temporary employment agencies: Temporary employment agencies are companies who train their employees on certain specific employment areas. Below are some advantages and disadvantages of these very agencies:

Advantages:

— Reduce overtime-turnover problem, recruitment, and hiring expenses

— Provide screened and trained qualified employees

— Create employee commitment through full-time position possibilities and benefits

— Ability to supply a complete harmonious work crew

Disadvantages:

— Charge Higher fees for temporary employees

— Temporary Employees tend to face integration problems

Employee referral programmes: These very programmes reward current employees who refer qualified applicants to the hotel.

SELECTING

Selecting means directly hiring the applicants or forwarding a hiring recommendation to top management. When selecting, the front office manager should seek the following skills:

— Mathematical aptitude

— Keyboard (typing) skills

Selection Tools

One of the most important selection tools is the job description which lists all tasks that makes up a work position, outlines reporting relationships, responsibilities, working conditions, equipment, and material to be used. The other vital selection tool is the job specification, which includes specific needs and skills to appropriately perform a certain task

Evaluating Applicants

While evaluating applicants, the front office manager should review all completed job application forms. Later, he/she should check all applicant references. Lastly, the front office manager shall interview all selected applicants.

INTERVIEWING

The interviewer should an objective judge of people and their qualifications, a positive role model, and a skillful communicator. Moreover, the interview should be held in a comfortable private setting, with few, if any, interruptions or disturbances.

Why do we need to conduct an interview?:

— In order to establish a basis for a working relationship

— In order to collect enough, accurate information to make an informal hiring decision

— In order to provide enough information to help the applicant make a decision

— In order to promote the company and the work position to the preferred applicant

— In order to create goodwill between the hotel and the applicant

Interview questions: Ask the applicant for a list rather than a single response, which allows for more spontaneity. Follow-up questions can be asked to narrow up the field. Use direct questions to verify facts and cover a lot of information quickly. A direct question is sometimes called a closed question and usually requires a simple answer, such as yes or no. Ask indirect or open ended questions, or ask the applicant to make comparisons. This technique is useful when the interviewer is seeking more than standard responses. An open-ended question is one that the applicant must elaborate on, such as "What were your favorite subjects in school?"

Pursue a specific subject in depth when a response seems unreasonable or unrealistic. Probe for additional information when the applicant gives a partial response. Restating the reply as a question usually does this, such as, "So you felt that the department was just too big, didn't you?". Use short affirmative responses to encourage the applicant to continue talking, such as, "I see," or "Please go on.", sometimes, it may also be helpful to nod your head in agreement. Use silence to indicate that the applicant should continue speaking. Suggest sample answers when the applicant does not understand the question. Vary applicant responses by making comments rather than always asking questions.

Interview evaluation: The applicant who scores the highest on the interview evaluation form will probably be selected. Moreover, when selecting an Applicant for a vacant position, the hotel shall inform all the other applicants that the position has been filled. Lastly, the human resource department should document all employee interviews even for the ones who are not accepted.

Staff Motivation

Maslow hierarchy of needs:

Self Actualisation

⇑

Self Esteem

⇑

Social Needs

⇑

Security Needs

⇑

Physical/Physiological Needs

Motivation in the front office: Motivation is the art of stimulating a front office staff member's interest in a particular job, project, or subject to the extent that he/she is challenged to be continuously attentive, observant, and committed. In order to motivate front office personnel, their human needs associated with personal worth, value, and belonging—needs to be satisfied. Employees in the front office department can be motivated in different ways such as:

Training

— In order to motivate front office staff, we need to train employees on "What to do?", "How to do?" and "Why tasks are done in certain ways?"

— Training of front office staff reduces the frustration the staff experiences when they do not know what is expected from them. Hence, makes staff more productive, efficient, and easier to manage.

— A very specific kind of training is cross training which means training the front office employees for more than 1 job.

Recognition

In order to motivate front office employees, the front office manager should recognise or appreciate certain staff members for their extraordinary work. This very recognition might stem from guests, management, and/or peers. In parallel, employees recognised shall receive some incentives.

Communication

In order to motivate front office staff, the hotel must keep them informed about all the upcoming events in the front office department. Some pieces of information communicated might include:

— Job opening announcements
— Promotion, transfer, resignation, and recruitment announcements
— New recruit announcements
— Special recognition awards
— Birthday, marriage, engagement, and birth announcements
— Upcoming event information

Incentive Programmes

Incentive programmes are designed to offer special recognition to employees who have met certain performance standards. The front office manager shall consider the following basic guidelines when developing an incentive programme:

— Develop an incentive programme that is appropriate and specific to the front office department
— Outline the specific goals and objectives for the incentive programme
— Define the conditions and requirements, which the front office staff must meet to receive recognition and rewards
— Brainstorm a variety of rewards and obtain the necessary approvals for any expenditure
— Determine the date and the time the programme will start. The incentive programme shall be educative, realistic and creative

A well-designed front office incentive programme should:

— Recognise and reward exceptional staff performance
— Increase staff productivity
— Demonstrate commitment to guest satisfaction
— Provide front office staff with feedback concerning goal attainment
— Concentrate on enhanced occupancy figures, room revenue, average room rate, and guest satisfaction

E- Performance appraisal: In order to motivate front office employees, we need to provide them formal, written feedback concerning their job performances. Moreover, the front office manager needs to identify the strengths and weaknesses in each member's performance and provide, jointly with employees, plans and actions for improvement and progress.

In fact, Performance appraisal gives the front office manager and each employee the opportunity to develop specific goals and progress dates. The front office manager shall recognise and reward outstanding performances through possible promotions, salary increases, and additional responsibilities.

9

FRONT OFFICE HOUSEKEEPING

The Housekeeping Department is one of the busiest sections in the hotel as far as the variety of functions performed, and number of staff working. It is usually situated at the laundry room or any other convenient place close to Housekeeping Supplies. The Housekeeping Department is responsible for:

— Neatness and Cleanliness of all guest rooms and most public areas

— Maintenance of recycled and non-recycled cleaning inventories

Some of the above mentioned functions might however be leased to a concessionaire. In this case, hotel shall still have a housekeeping department but to a minimum number of staff! The housekeeping department is headed by an executive housekeeper. The procedure of cleaning guest rooms by the housekeeping department can be summarized in the following way:

— Checkout clerk (or cashier) contacts the Housekeeping Department that a room became vacant and needs cleaning!

— Housekeeping Department updates the room status from occupied to on-change and sends a room maid to clean the room

— Room maid cleans the room and contacts the housekeeping department back about the latest status and condition of the room (especially for out-of-order and out-of-service!)

— If the room is out of order for any reason (i.e. Room is extensively dirty, or needs repair!), then the housekeeping department deducts that room from those available for sale, until either scheduled to be extensively cleaned or post to the confirmation from the Maintenance Department that the deficiency was repaired!

— Housekeeping department sends their inspectors to check whether the stated room has been cleaned to the hotel standards or not!

— If the room is cleaned to hotel's standards, the housekeeping department shall update the room status from on-change to clean and available for sale and communicate this to the front office department!

- If the room is not cleaned to hotel standards, inspectors communicate to the housekeeping department that the room shall be cleaned again!

The main two important areas where collaboration is vital between the housekeeping and front office department are listed below:

— Have always clean rooms for expected arrivals and stayovers

— Satisfy special guest needs as far as amenities and facilities requested in their rooms are concerned

Process of Cleaning and Inspection

The room status for each room determines how much effort, time, labor, and hence scheduled staff is needed by the housekeeping department on any shift. The housekeeping department shall first clean rooms for expected arrivals first, then stayover rooms and eventually vacant rooms! The reason is that rooms for new arrivals takes more time to be cleaned to hotel standards again and that guests might come any time to request their rooms even before the pre-determined beginning of check-in time!

That's why; the housekeeping department shall be communicated from the reservation department on a daily basis expected arrival, stayover, and departure lists to be able to schedule the optimum number of room maids and inspectors for the expected business volume! Moreover, cleaning procedure of guest rooms, there should be a communication between the front office department and housekeeping department to be able to communicate the recent room status of each room! This communication is vital because nobody would like to make a guest wait in the lobby because his/her room is not yet clean or due to the fact that the housekeeping department did not communicate on real time the status to the front office!

Lastly, the housekeeping department shall ensure that every room maid shall use efficiently most of his valuable time in cleaning not in going back and forth in the corridors! Yet, since some hotels might operate under the manual or Semi-automated systems, some delays and hence, problems might occur! To illustrate, let's consider the guest room cleaning process along with the different operating modes under which a hotel might operate:

Manual System

Under this system, due to the fact that room maids shall first clean rooms for new arrival, then stayover rooms and at last vacant rooms, these very cleaning personnel have two ways to do it:

— Post to cleaning each room, go to the housekeeping department, inform them about the status and then come back to clean the next room. This would solve the potential problem that a guest might be waiting for a clean room due to a communication of the housekeeping department not in real tome! However this would decrease the number of rooms cleaned and inspected by room maids and inspectors, which would mean higher housekeeping labor costs!

— Post to cleaning certain category of rooms, and/or all rooms, room maids inform the housekeeping department, and then inspectors would inspect all rooms, at the same time, inform the department about the recent statuses! This would increase maids' and inspectors' efficiency but would cause guests waiting in the lobby to be escorted to their rooms!

Semi-automated System

Under this system, room maids and inspectors might use either a phone machine situated at the center of each corridor, or pagers and beepers to communicate the recent room status. This proved to be efficient as to minimize labor cost and the time that a guest spends on the lobby waiting to be escorted to his/her room! However, this might create some problems:

— Upon the usage of beepers, the housekeeping department doesn't know exactly which room is cleaned or inspected, therefore will spend needless time to be certain which would put more stress on check-in personnel to convince a waiting guest in the lobby area!

— Guests tend to be both not at ease and dissatisfied seeing hotel personnel in their rooms using beepers and might think that something wrong happened in their rooms!

Fully Automated System

This is the best system, which eliminates nearly all time losses spent by room maids and inspectors, to inform the housekeeping department and the time needed to be spent needlessly at the lobby area! Under this very system, each room maid and inspector, prior to the fulfillment of his or her duties in the room, can send a coded message from the guest's room telephone to the housekeeping department. Later an electronic message can be send automatically to check-in personnel confirming that the room is cleaned to standards and waiting for the next arrival!

Room Status

The front office and the housekeeping department shall prepare at the same time, as frequent as needed by management, their room status reports, which lists, according to each department, the recent room status of each room in the hotel. Later, these two reports shall be cross-referenced and compared to detect room status discrepancies and correct them as soon as possible in order to maximize room revenue, detect skippers before it is too late. In the manual system, room status reports shall be reconciled at least each hour. This very frequency might increase as the business volume increases.

In the semi-automated system, reconciliation shall be at least once per shift (preferably at the beginning of each shift)! Lastly under the fully automated system, since housekeeping and front office department's communication is ensured electronically on real time, reconciliation needs to be done only at the night shift by the night auditor!

If at the reservation or registration process, guests have communicated certain specific needs related to certain specific amenities and/or facilities that needed to be provided in the room, then the front office department shall communicate this directly to the Housekeeping department or indirectly to the concierge who shall further communicate this to the housekeeping department and follow up to ensure the actual provision in a timely and accurate manner!

10

CLIENT ENTERTAINING

INVITATIONS

Invitations can be anything from a informal spontaneous request asking someone to come over to your place for dinner to a formal invitations to a ball or a wedding. The first kind of invitation is generally done on the phone or in person while the other is elegantly printed and mailed. Invitations to a ball a wedding or any official functions do not carry any "return" obligations. Invitations to private parties at home do carry a return obligation. In case you are an invitee to a large cocktail party it means that next time you host a party of a similar nature your host and hostess must be your guest list. But if you have been invited to a small dinner party then it should be returned in kind within a couple of months.

You are no way obliged to accept an invitation, but if you do accept you must go. Nothing can change the acceptance to a regret except a sudden illness, a death in the family or a sudden trip. Also make sure that after refusing an invitation don't go to another party on the same day. When giving out invitations make sure to give a copy to all the guest and not by leaving out your close friends and invite them verbally.

Formal invitations are always made on white or cream cards. The choice of language should be conservative. When you wish your guest to do formally dressed make sure you mention it on the invitation card. In case you don't want the invitation to be engraved, it can be hand written but never typed. Invitations to a dinner party must be handed out at least two to three weeks before time. Titles are always sued or formal invitations. Answer or response cards it should be small and engraved in the same style as the invitation itself.

— *Maps*—to the location of the party.

— Tickets/raffle tickets—Any tickets that would be needed during the course of the party should also be enclosed.

Acceptance or regret: The form of acceptance or regret depends on the kind of invitation. A formal invitation will be replied by a formal note. The reply is always addressed to the person who sends the invitation. In case the invitation is for two people and only one person will be able to attend, then regret can be combined with acceptance.

Invitation cards that are informal can be made on visiting cards or readymade fill in cards or informal folded cards on which the matter can be written On most informal occasions invitation is generally made over the phone or person. A reply to an informal invitation will be informal. One should never ask for an invitation for oneself or others. In case you can't go for a party because you have guests staying over with you, you tell your hostess so and then if she asks you to bring them along, it's perfectly fine.

For changing your answer from "yes" to "no" and vice versa you should inform your host immediately. In case you have decided not to go for a party for a fixed number of people like a seated dinner and you change your decision. It is nest not to go for the party as you will be embarrassing your host.

Entertaining at Home

First consideration when you entertain at home is the space you have available for entertaining, and the degreed of formality you can and want to achieve. A person staying in a large house can throw a formal dinner party while a person staying in a small house with a large deck or a patio can throw a barbe-que party. There are certain requisites for a successful dinner party. They are:

- — Guests who are congenial
- — A menu that is well planned and suited the guests taste
- — An attractive table
- — Food that is well prepared
- — Servants who are competent and pleasant
- — A gracious and cordial hostess and host

While making a guest list make sure that the guests mix very well with each other and are interesting to each other. As the guests enter they should be greeted at the door and welcomed very warmly. Pay equal attention to all your guests and socialise with everyone. In case any guest is late, fifteen minutes is the accepted time to wait for after the official dinner time. The guests of honour are always seated to the right of the host and the hostess. They wait for all the guests to be seated before seating themselves. While seating, ensure that there is an equal dispersion of male and female guests. Always ensure that the ladies are seated before the gents are.

Service of food: Is always done coursewise. Never should all the items in the menu put together on the table in the beginning itself, except in case of a buffet. Always a second helping should be offered to all the guests. When cleaning the table ensure that the dished are never scarped at the table, two dishes should be carried in at time.

Inerbriated guests: When a guest gets obnoxious or embarrassing at your party, take the help of those whom he has come with to get him home or to help him if he is felling sick. If he insults anyone else at your party, make sure you pacify the insulted person and help the drunk person home or to the bedroom. Never let a drunk person get behind the wheel or the car.

If the guests decide to stay on longer at the party than what you had hoped for, the best way to end the party would be to close the bar and remove all the drinks. Still if some people continue to stay on it would be bets to make the excuse that you have to go out somewhere else and some one else is expecting you.

Grooming: Whatever occasion you have been invited to you should dress for the occasion. If a dress code has been specified, make sure you stick to it. Do not be obnoxious and loud. If you are visiting a friend you should wear what you are most comfortable with. In case you are not sure of what to wear it is all right to call up your host and ask him what to wear.

At a dance party a man must dance with his hostess, and must dance the firs and the last dances with the woman he bought to the party. When making the guest list for such a party. When making the guest list for such a party, make sure you have equal number of males and females.

Advice for Guests, Hosts and Hostesses

Never arrive early: Try to be as close to the time given on the invitation as possible. In case, in certain localities, coming late is an accepted norm it is best to follow it.

Gifts for the hostess: When a party is thrown especially for you, you should send the hostess some flowers beforehand. Other guests need not do this but may however, send flowers or a thank you note the next day. Taking wine as a gift for a small dinner party is now an accepted norm.

Helping your hostess

Single woman—in case you have a couple coming that way ask them to pick up and drop her. In case you are single and you have been invited for a party you will be showing a single lady great consideration by asking her to come with you. No matter how much you want to help the hostess or to keep company, do not follow her to the kitchen and chat her away. When she is passing a dish around or when she is clearing the table do not get in her way by jumping up to help her unless she has asked you before hand. When a butler or a servant is serving you, do not try to help.

After dinner: Guests do not place their napkins on the table until the hostess does so. When she rises to signal the end of the meal, do not continue to sit down and prolong your conversation.

Departing: Once you have decided to go and have said so to the other guests, do so. Be sensitive enough to understand that the party has come to an end. In case you are the guest of honour leave early enough so that you don't delay the others. Do not leave immediately after dinner, it is polite to wait for at least an hour after dinner. If you have gone to the party in someone else's car it is up to them to decide when to go.

Uninvited guest—other than the normal requirement of being courteous to the guest you have no other special obligation towards him. You may spend some time with him if you are free. If you cannot feed anther person you could ask him to drop by later.

Liquor problem—to keep control over the bar pour the drinks yourself. Always insist on the use of a jigger. Do not provide drinks to drunken guests.

Toasts

Quiet frequently guests are called on to make a toast. The best solution is to say exactly what you feel. In case you are taken by surprise, you could just toast to the person's health. Or say something like "to----, God bless him", To appear more poised and eloquent, you could just adds a reminiscence praise or, a relevant story or joke. A touch of humour is rarely out of side. Before the toast a glass of wine or champagne may be passed around. Non drinkers may just pick up an empty glass. The glass need not be drained, a sip will suffice.

It is extremely discourteous to remain seated during a toast. One must rise and join in the spirit. The person being seated does not stand or drink to the toast. He replies to the toast by saying thank you or proposing a return toast. A lady's reply to a toast is generally only a smile and a nod of the head or she may just raise her glass towards the person making the toast.

Entertain at a Restaurant

Showing courtesy towards the restaurant owner. Never change your mind about going to a restaurant where you have made a reservation without calling to let them know. After all, they have your table and turned away other paying customer on your behalf. If you hope to be a regular customer this quickest way to lose your welcome. Be on time for your reservation. Many popular restaurants have two seating, and they count on you being on time.

If you show up at 8:30 for a 6.45 reservation, you deserve to be turned away. You will have cost the restaurant money by removing the possibility of two seating at your table that night. If the number of people in your party change from the rime you made the reservation, call to advise them of the new number. The restaurant must move tables and chairs around to accommodate you, and this takes time. They need this information as soon as possible.

Host and the Restaurant Manners

On the morning of your lunch, make two telephone calls:

— To reconfirm your reservation with the restaurant.

— To reconfirm with your guest

Always arrive at the restaurant before your guests. It's lonely and embarrassing for you guest to arrive punctually and be obliged to stand for lonely in a crowded restaurant foyer, wondering where you are and if he or she should wait outside. Make it clear, before you meet, that you are paying the bill. As soon as you have issued the invitation and received an affirmative reply, take charge.

Settle the time, place and date. The entire warm mood of the occasion is ruined when people argue over the bill and grapple for it at the end of the meal. If you are taking a person to a place with a strict dress code, communicate it before the date, so that your guest won't turn up in embarrassingly inappropriate clothing. Always give your guests the best seats at the table. An especially heavy or disabled guest should have an outside seat, not a banquette, from which it is difficult to enter and exit.

Have your guest order first and help him or her in case of difficulty with a foreign menu. Always make certain that your guest is served first. Even if you do not drink, offer your guest a pre-meal drink as well as wine with the meal. If you are dining with your spouses who do not work with you, avoid discussing business all the time. It's natural to discuss matters of mutual business interest, but half the conversation should be non-business oriented, in deference to the people at the table who are not involved in your affairs.

Your manners really show when you are a guest in a private home. Treat the staff graciously. Guest whoever greets you at the front door onwards. Don't be a snooper in the house. It is appallingly bad taste to open your host's medicine cabinet, or go through your hostess's closets, and the like. Don't go on your own house tour. If your hosts urge you to accompany them on a tour, or to " wander around by your self fine but don't go off without authorisation. That's snooping. Stay out of your host's kitchen. You may want to see what kind of range and refrigerator she has, or you may have heard you boss has just had her kitchen redesigned. Wait until you see it in a magazine: and let the party staff do their job.

There are ways to limit the number of gifts we all give and receive. But there are still occasions when they are mandatory. There are categories of gifts that are appropriate for many different occasions and events.

Gifts of money: Although giving money is sometime a lazy way of avoiding the trouble of choosing a gift, there are occasion when a check is the most welcome present of all. For people who dislike the idea of a check or cash, a gift certificate is a very appropriate gift. When a greet number of checks or gifts of cash are received as at a wedding reception or a big anniversary party, the envelopes need not be opened at the time. At smaller parties, or when just a few envelopes are given, the recipient opens them and thanks them but does not mention the amount in front of the others.

Flowers: Flowers may be sent by almost everyone to almost anyone. There are certain times when sending them is obligatory. These occasions include funerals, debutantes parties, dinners at private homes and other where local customs demand it. Flowers make the best gifts for a dinner hostess. Ideally, they should be sent ahead of time, so that the hostess may have them on display when the guest arrives if you are taking them with you, it is best to have them already arranged so that your hostess does not have to leave her guests to put them in a container.

When you are a guest of honour at a dinner party, you should send the hostess a flower arrangement the day of the party. For many years flowers were not considered an appropriate gift for men. In the recent years, however, the attitude has changed for and men who are not longer ashamed to show their appreciation for beauty, gift to a man who is ill, opening a new office or a birthday.

Birth stones as gifts: Jewellery containing birthstones are lovely birthday presents. Birthstones are also used as a substitute for the diamonds in engagement rings. For silver wedding anniversaries, it is very appropriate to give gifts in silver. It blends with the theme of the occasion.

In some areas a gift is taken to a host or hostess who has extended an invitation for dinner. Gifts need not be taken to large cocktail parties or receptions unless it is to honour an occasion. Gifts may be flowers, home-made cookies or jam, a box of candy, bottles of wine, liquor or liqueurs, If gifts of food are taken, it should be made clear that they are not intended for the meal being served. It is obligatory that who spend a weekend or longer take a gift for the host and the hostess. The length of the visit and the elaborateness of the entertainment determine the elaborateness of the gift. You may take the host and the hostess our for dinner or to another entertainment or take the timing for one evening meal which you prepare and serve as a thank you for their hospitality.

Half the fun of giving and receiving present at any party is to see and enjoy what everyone has brought. The nicest way to do this is to have all the presents collected in place until everyone has arrived, at which time the guest of honour opens them. Whether a gift is an inexpensive gag present of a more expensive article is not important. The recipient reads the cards enclosed, particularly if they are funny ones, and show enthusiasm for each gift. It is important to include a card even with a gift you deliver personally because many people like to collect them and save the cards they receive at these times as mementos of the occasion.

On occasions when gifts are not necessarily expected but two or three people bring them regardless, they are opened in the donor presence but without drawing the attention of the other guests. When an invitation says 'No Gifts Please' the request should be honoured. If you are very close to the sender, or the guest of honour, you may take or send a gift to his or her home before of after the party. But to take it to the celebration is only embarrassing to the host or the hostess and rude to the guests who have complied with the request.

KEV CARDS—(ARRIVAL CARDS) OR BOOKLETS:

Either a small card or booklet, which is given to each guest on arrival, the Hotel Receptionist fills in the following details:

— Room Number

— Room rate per night (plus or including VAT)

— Number of nights guest is due to stay date) for departure

These arrival/key cards were first introduced for security reasons, for example, when a guest requested his key from either the hall porter or the Receptionist, he was first obliged to show his key card, as proof that he was staying in the hotel, and to ensure that he was in fact requesting the correct room number. In many hotels guests are obliged to show this key card, when he wishes to charge an item to his account, for example in the Restaurant, the guest is requested to sign his bill, and the waiter will ask to see the card, and write the room number on the bill (if the guest has not already done so). These cards or booklets vary from hotel to hotel, and other information draws the attention of the guest to the following:

— Policy of hotel regarding valuables

— Payment of accounts

— Fire

And many other details of amenities which the hotel offers, plus some adverts of local interest, which may help to pay for the cost of producing these cards or booklets.

11

Planning and Evaluation

Management Functions

— *Planning*: At the planning stage, the front office manager shall determine the department's goals. Later, the front office manager shall use these goals as a guide for planning more specific and measurable objectives. Lastly, the front office manager shall determine the strategies and tactics to reach these objectives.

— *Organising*: The front office manager shall organise the work to be done through dividing it among staff members. While doing so, the work shall be distributed fairly and shall be completed in a timely manner.

— *Coordinating*: Involves bringing together and using the available resources to attain planned goals.

— *Staffing*: Involves recruiting applicants, selecting those best qualifies for positions, and scheduling employees.

— *Leading*: Involves overseeing, motivating, training, disciplining, and setting an example for the front office.

— *Controlling*: Ensures that the actual results of operations closely match planned results.

— *Evaluating*: Determines the extent to which planned goals are, in fact, attained. Moreover, it involves reviewing and, when necessary, revising or helping to revise front office goals.

Room Rates Establishment

The front office manager shall assign to each room category a rack rate. In accordance, front office employees are expected to sell rooms at rack unless a guest qualifies for an alternative room rate (ex: corporate or commercial rate, group rate, promotional rate, incentive rate, family rate, day rate, package plan rate, complementary rate...). While establishing room rates, management shall be careful about its operating costs, inflationary factors, and competition. Generally, there are three popular approaches to pricing rooms:

— Market condition approach

— Rule-of-thumb approach

— Hubbart formula approach

Market condition approach: Under this very approach, management shall look at comparable hotels in the geographical market, see what they are charging for the same product, and "charge only what the market will accept". Some drawbacks of this approach are that it does not take into consideration the value of the property, and what a strong sales effort may accomplish.

Rule of thumb approach: In this very approach, the rate of a room shall be $ 1 for each $ 1,000 of construction and furnishing cost per room, assuming a 70% occupancy rate. This approach, however, fails to take into consideration the inflation term, the contribution of other facilities and services towards the hotel's desired profitability, and assumes a certain level of occupancy rate.

Hubbart formula approach: This very approach considers operating costs, desired profits, and expected number of rooms sold (i.e. demand). The procedure of calculating a room rate is as follows:

— Calculate the hotel's desired profit by multiplying the desired rate of return (ROI) by the owner's investment.

— Calculate pre-tax profits by dividing the desired profit by 1 minus hotel's tax rate.

— Calculate fixed charges and management fees. This calculation includes estimating depreciation, interest expense, property taxes, insurance, amortisation, building mortgage, land, rent, and management fees.

— Calculate undistributed operating expenses. This includes estimating administrative and general expenses, data processing expenses, human resources expenses, transportation expenses, marketing expenses, property operation and maintenance expenses, and energy costs.

— Estimate non-room operating department income or loss, that is, F&B department income or loss, telephone department income or loss.

— Calculate the required room department income which is the sum of pre-tax profits, fixed charges and management fees, undistributed operating expenses, and other operating department losses less other department incomes.

— Determine the rooms department revenue which is the required room department income, plus other room department direct expenses of payroll and related expenses, plus other direct operating expenses.

— Calculate the average room rate by dividing rooms department revenue by the expected number of rooms to be sold.

Forecasting Room Availability

Forecasting room availability is forecasting the number of rooms available for sale on any future date. This type of forecasting helps manage the reservation process, guides the front office staff for an effective rooms management, and can be used as an occupancy forecast, which is, further, useful in attempting to schedule the necessary number of employees for an expected volume of business. In order to forecast room availability, the following data are needed:

— Number of expected room arrivals

— Number of expected room walk-ins

— Number of expected room stayovers

— Number of expected room no-shows

— Number of expected room understays

— Number of expected room check-outs

— Number of expected room overstays

These data help the front office in conduct various daily operational ratios such as:

— No-shows percentage = (number of no-show rooms)/(number of rooms reserved)

— Walk-ins percentage = (number of walk-in rooms)/(total number of rooms arrivals)

— Overstays percentage = (number of overstay rooms)/(number of expected check-outs)

— Understays percentage = (number of understay rooms)/(number of expected check-outs)

The forecasted number of rooms available for sale for any future date can be tracked using the following formula:

> Forecasted number of rooms available for sale = total number of guest rooms - number of out of order rooms - number of stayovers rooms - number of reserved rooms +

number of no-show rooms + number of understay rooms - number of overstay rooms

Under non-automated and semi-automated systems, number of rooms available for sale forecasts are calculated upon demand and need and vary from three-day to ten-day forecasts. However, under fully automated systems, forecasts can be done at any moment for any future period of time. For, computers run forecasts on a room count considerations, hence eliminating tedious labour work and human error margins.

BUDGETING FOR OPERATIONS

At least once per year, hotels shall prepare annual budgets, which are profit plans that address all revenue sources and expense items for the following calendar year. Moreover, the hotel annual operating budget represents standards against which management can evaluate actual results of operations. In the annual budget preparation process, close coordination efforts of all management personnel is vital. The hotel's annual operation budget is commonly divided into monthly plans, which in turn are divided into weekly and even daily plans, for better control over actual results.

While preparing the front office department annual budget, the front office manager shall coordinate with the accounting department as to estimate only rooms revenue and related direct expenses. The hotel controller and the general manager, then, shall revise this very budget.

— *Forecasting room revenue*: In order to forecast room revenue, the front office manager might consult historical financial information such as past room revenue, past number of rooms sold, past average daily rate, and past occupancy rates.

— *Forecasting direct expenses*: Due to the fact front office manager is responsible only for his/her department direct expenses (i.e. variable costs), the front office manager can, also, consult historical financial data depicting variable cost to room revenue ratios, in order to estimate department expenses.

— *Refining budget plans*: Sometimes, if external uncontrollable factors change significantly, in an unexpected way, then the actual operating budgeted figures shall be revised.

FRONT OFFICE OPERATIONS EVALUATION

A successful front office manager shall continuously evaluate the results of department activities on a daily, monthly, quarterly, and yearly basis. While evaluating, the following items and tools shall be used:

— Daily operations report
— Occupancy ratios
— Rooms revenue analysis
— Hotel income statement
— Rooms division income statement or schedule
— Rooms division budgets report
— Operating ratios and ratio standards

Daily operations report: It is also known as the manager's report, the daily report, and the daily revenue report. This very report contains a summary of the hotel's financial activities during a 24-Hour period. Moreover, it serves as to reconcile cash, bank accounts, and revenue and accounts receivable, and as an important data that must be input to link front and back office computer functions.

Occupancy ratios: Occupancy ratios measure the success of the front office in selling the hotel's primary product (i.e. guestrooms). Some common ratios used in the front office department are given below:

— Occupancy percentage = (number of rooms occupied) / (total number of rooms available for sale)

— Multiple occupancy percentage = (number of rooms occupied by more than one guest) / (total number of rooms occupied)

— Average guests per rooms sold = (total number of guests) / (total number of rooms sold)

— Average daily rate = (total rooms revenue) / (total number of rooms sold)

— Average rate per guest = (total rooms revenue) / (total number of guests)

Rooms revenue analysis: One main report to enhance control over room revenue is the room rate variance report, which is the one that lists those rooms that have been sold at rates other than their rack rates. Another form is the yield statistic, which is the ratio of the actual revenue to the total possible potential revenue if all rooms are sold at rack rates. Yield statistic = (actual room revenue) / (potential room revenue)

Hotel income statement: This very statement provides important financial information about the results of hotel operations for a given period of time

Rooms division income statement: The rooms division income statement (sometimes called a schedule) shall be referenced on the hotel's income statement. Moreover, the rooms division schedule shall be prepared by hotel's accounting division not the hotel's front office accounting staff.

Rooms division budget reports: These reports are monthly budget forms that compare actual revenue and expense figures against budgeted amounts depicted both in dollar values and percentage variances

Operating ratios: Operating ratios (ex. occupancy ratios, yield statistic.) assist managers in evaluating the success of front office operations. Moreover, for ratios to be meaningful they should be compared against proper standards such as prior period's, competitor's, and/or budgeted ratios.

12

OFFICE ORGANISATION

When undertaking a large project, it makes sense to first address the largest aspects, get those pieces in place, and then move to the smaller, more detailed aspects of the project. A bit of planning on the front end sets you up for success in any project, whether you are painting a landscape or organising your office. In an office setting, there are large framework factors to consider before you get down to the nitty-gritty detail work of organising the drawers, nooks, and crannies in your office.

You learn how to organise and decorate your office space (based on its size), choose the appropriate furniture for your space and needs, select the flooring style that works best for you, and decide upon the proper colour scheme and lighting for your working style and profession. Because you spend so much time in your office, it's important that you feel comfortable and enjoy your time there.

CHOOSING PRIMARY FURNITURE

Primary furniture consists of your desk, work surfaces, and your chair. Secondary furniture is anything additional, such as filing cabinets, conference tables, guest chairs, or shelving units. Your primary furniture is one of the most important elements in your office. Your desk serves as a place for working, as well as storage of Zone One items, and it is the keystone of your office.

Your chair is the tool you use most in conjunction with your desk and it is equally important. If your office has been furnished by your current employer, you might have had no choice about the furniture in your office when you took your job. If it isn't working for you, however, it is in your best interest-and ultimately the company's best interest-to replace it with furniture that works for you.

If you're self-employed, it's even more important because any time you're nonproductive you're losing income. When thinking about your office furniture, you'll need to remember to create dedicated space for working at your computer, doing administrative or other paper work, and completing various projects.

Choosing a Desk and Desktop Storage

The way you work and the items and information in your office determines the style of desk you need. If your work is paper-intensive and your projects require a large amount of flat work space, consider using a desk with a return. A return is the second piece of furniture that makes a desk L-shaped, as shown in Figure 1. This additional piece is used to add extra work space.

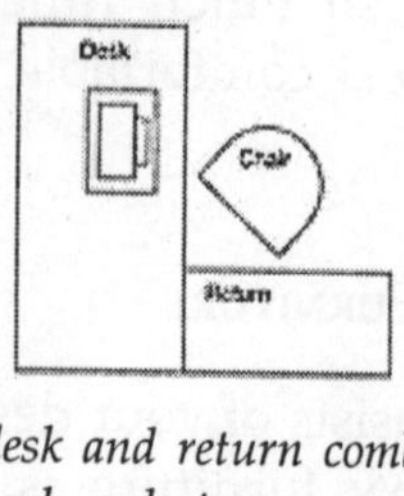

Figure 1. An L-shaped desk and return combination offers additional work and storage space

If your work requires you to refer to books, manuals, or other reference materials, consider purchasing a desk with a hutch on top for storing those items close at hand. A hutch is a great way to keep materials nearby without losing any of your work surface. Figure 2 shows a desk with a hutch that includes two rows of shelves.

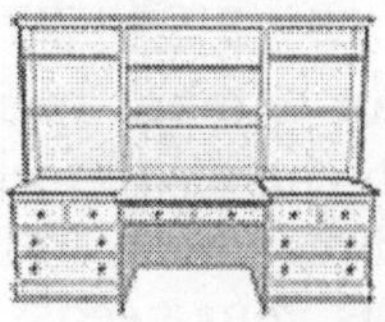

Figure 2. The hutch above the desk offers extra storage for items used frequently and needed close at hand

If you work from a cubicle, you might not have the ability to add a hutch to your desk. However, many desks situated in cubes automatically come with closed overhead cabinet space. This additional storage is great for keeping reference materials, books, and binders nearby without losing any work space on your desktop.

There are also desks that fit across the corner of a room, as shown in Figure 3. Corner desks give you the option to place a hutch on top in the center. A corner desk is a great way to utilize a small office, while still leaving space for additional furniture in the center or other side of the room.

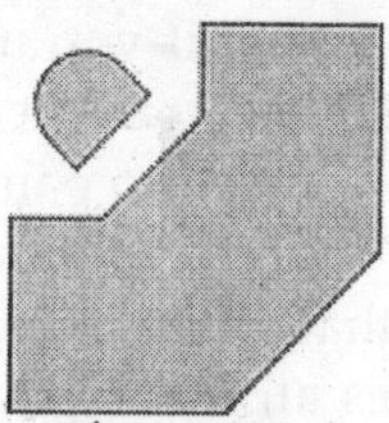

Figure 3. A corner desk creates open space in the center of the office for traffic flow.

Selecting Right Office Chair

The chair you choose is important, especially if you spend most of your time in your office, rather than out in the field. A quality desk chair that fits you well will make a big difference in the way your body feels at the end of each day, which contributes either positively or negatively to your effectiveness and productivity.

Never buy a chair without spending several minutes sitting in it first. Each chair will feel different to you, and before you spend a dime you want to be sure the chair is comfortable and meets your needs. Be sure the chair you choose has several options for adjustment. You should easily be able to change the height of the seat and back, as well as the armrests. Many chairs offer adjustable tension settings on the backrest that enable you to determine how much pressure it takes to recline. Check for adjustable lumbar settings as well, so you can set the chair to support your lower back comfortably.

Set the overall height of your chair so you can comfortably use your mouse and keyboard when working at the computer. If you can't put your feet on the floor when your chair is at the proper height, consider getting something to rest your feet on. Using a footrest reduces muscle fatigue by taking pressure off your lower back and will keep pressure off the back of your legs.

The bottom line is that if you use an office chair that doesn't offer you adequate comfort and support, you are needlessly subjecting yourself to pain and stress that could easily be avoided. It's worth spending extra money on a higher-quality chair that will eliminate the back pain and other physical stresses an inadequate chair could cause.

— Create a scale drawing of your office

— Learn to achieve maximum function with minimum furniture

— Plan for traffic flow and place furniture accordingly
— Place office equipment and peripherals

Scale Model to Lay Out Your Office

It's important to know how much actual space you have to work with before you jump into creating (or re-creating) your office. Keep in mind that you're striving to create a comfortable work space with good traffic flow. Looking through catalogs and finding items you love is the easy part. If you don't know how much room you're working with, however, you could spend a lot of money on furniture that doesn't work for you.

Buying first and measuring later means your furniture might end up being too large or too small for the room. This is why it's worth taking a little time to make a basic scale drawing of your room. The scale drawing gives you a great foundation from which to begin adding and moving office furniture. Using a scale-model floor plan and paper cutouts of furniture and equipment is the best way to try out different plans before you commit to one. Plus, you avoid hauling furniture around the room, trying various configurations until you get it right. Moving paper cutouts is a whole lot easier than moving furniture. You'll Need

— Tape measure
— Graph paper
— Mechanical pencil
— Ruler or other straight-edge device
— Scissors
— Sticky notes

Measuring and Creating Scale Drawings

A scale model or scale drawing is a rendition of something

large, reduced in size but proportionally accurate. To create a drawing of your office, measure the space using a tape measure. To get the most accurate measurements for your scale drawing, measure the entire length of each wall first, noting it on paper, and then measure across the room to double-check your numbers.

After you have your measurements written down, use your graph paper and mathematically figure out how many squares you want to be equivalent to one foot. Choose this ratio based on the overall size of your graph paper and the drawing size you'll need in order to sketch in furniture and equipment placement.

Let's say your room is 20′ x 14′ and you are using graph paper with 1/4" squares. A scale of 1/2" (two squares) to a foot means that a 20-foot wall would convert to a 10-inch line on your paper. Using a scale of 1/2" to a foot gives you plenty of room to write and makes the drawing large enough to easily see each element. If your room is relatively small, go ahead and use a larger scale of 1" per foot.

Even though you won't need to write anything more than the names of each item and its dimensions, the larger you make your scale, the more room you'll have to make these notes on the floor plan. After you've chosen your scale, be sure to note it somewhere on the paper so you can remember it later. For example, jot a note on the floor plan that says, "One inch = one foot."

Now that you've chosen your scale, draw the outline of your room using your graph paper and straight edge. After you have drawn the lengths of the walls on your graph paper, measure and draw in the locations of the door openings and windows; also indicate on your drawing where the phone jacks and outlets are located.

Remember to draw your window and door openings to scale so you can accurately see how everything fits together on paper. The scale drawing in Figure 4 shows a 14' x 16' office drawn on graph paper using two squares for each linear foot. The doors, windows, outlets, and jacks have been added to scale in this drawing.

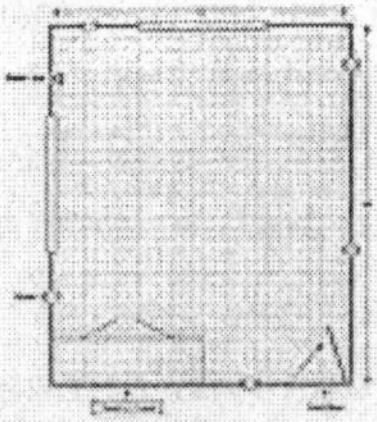

Figure 4. This drawing shows the added elements of windows, doors, closet space, outlets (which are shown as a circle with two lines intersecting), and phone jacks (which are shown as triangles).

It is helpful to look through magazines to find photos of offices that inspire you. You certainly don't need to replicate any one office, but you can choose specific elements from each photo you like and combine them to make your space new and unique. Now that you have your physical space outlined to scale on graph paper, you're ready to move on to the next step, which is considering the furniture layout of your office.

Creating Furniture Cutouts

Now you're ready to begin testing office arrangements using paper cutouts to represent your primary office furnishings. Cutting out scale models of your furniture gives you an easy way to rearrange the elements of the room without doing any hard work. The beauty of it is you don't have to guess what it will look like or how much space you'll have left over because your model is created to tell you those things by virtue of the fact that it is built to scale.

Make your paper cutouts by measuring your present furniture, converting that measurement to the scale you've chosen for your drawing, and then cutting its shape to that size out of a sticky note. To convert actual size furniture to a cutout, just refer to your scale. Using a scale of 1/2" equals 1', a desk 5' by 2' would convert to a paper cutout of 2 1/2" by 1". Cut the model out of the sticky note, write the word desk on it and write the desk dimensions on the cutout as well. Be sure to use the sticky end of the note when cutting out your shape so it will stick to the graph.

When you place this two-dimensional scale model of your desk on your graph floor plan, you'll see how it looks exactly in proportion to the size of the room. Converting real objects to scale paper cutouts is very simple using basic math skills and a ruler. Repeat this process with each primary piece of furniture you have or want to place in your office. If you know you'll be replacing a piece of furniture or you plan to buy a piece and don't know its specific dimensions, cut out a scale model that approximates the size of the piece you plan to purchase.

This scale drawing exercise will be right up your alley. Take the time to do it, even though it takes a little while. With your strong visual leanings, the model will make it especially easy for you to imagine and plan your new space before you purchase new furniture or begin doing any heavy work.

Laying Out Your Furniture

Experiment on paper with different configurations for your furniture and you'll undoubtedly begin seeing the difference between effective and ineffective furniture layouts. In this section, we'll look at some sample layouts and discuss some of the pros and cons of each. Here are some criteria of effective office layout:

— The furnishings are in proportion to the size of the room.

— There is plenty of room for walking between furniture.

— The primary office chair has plenty of room to swivel and roll forward and backward. A good rule of thumb is a minimum of 18" between the back of the chair and the wall.

— Computer equipment, peripherals, and other machines are easily accessible from your seated position, without requiring you to reach or stretch.

— All doors should be clear of obstructions.

— You can walk straight into the room without running into anything or having to quickly turn to avoid a piece of furniture.

— Traffic patterns between frequently used items are short and straight whenever possible.

— Seating configuration creates comfortable conversation areas.

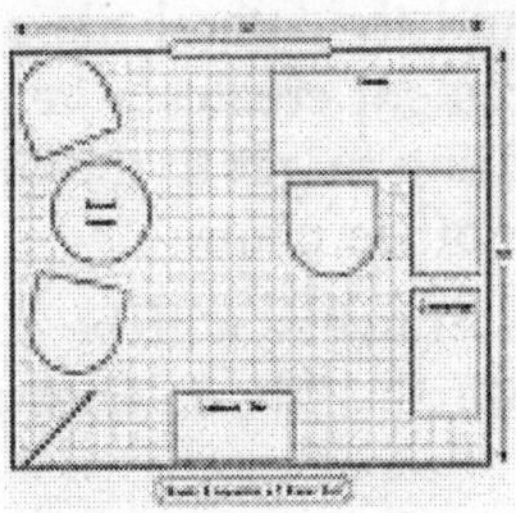

Figure 5. Facing directly out a window is appealing at first glance, but sitting with your back to the door can be unsettling for many people.

Initially it might seem like a great idea to have the desk set up so you can look outside all day, as in the preceding example. That would be a wonderful way to increase the enjoyment of the space. Several flaws exist in this layout, however:

— The position of the desk and chair puts your back to the door, which is a physically and psychologically weak position. When you can't see the door, visitors can easily enter your room and startle you. This vulnerability can create a subtle, underlying uneasiness that affects your focus.

— The guest chairs and small table inhibit an easy traffic flow upon entering the office.

— The position of the guest chairs and small table make it virtually impossible to use both chairs.

— The credenza in this position also creates a virtually unusable dead corner to its right, where clutter is likely to accumulate.

— The lateral file is too close to the door. It inhibits movement as you enter the office.

Figure 6 shows the same office space as Figure 5, with all the same furnishings. This time the desk is facing the door, which is a better working position. Several things are still wrong with this layout:

— The credenza and the lateral file are both behind the desk. This placement creates a very narrow walkway for anyone wanting to get to the desk and cramps the mobility of the office chair.

— The lateral file drawers will be difficult to open all the way because the file cabinet is too close to the chair.

— The guest chair is too close to the wall beside it, restricting movement.

— The traffic flow in this office is impeded. Every path you follow leads to a dead end. The closed end of each traffic path is unsettling. Many people will often avoid a space rather than feel trapped with only one way out.

— As you enter this room, you nearly walk into the guest chair to the right of the door. It is too close to the natural traffic pattern.

— The room is unbalanced. It feels "heavy" on the right side of the room and there is nothing to meet your eye as you walk through the door.

— The large empty space on the left is completely unused, making it a likely place for clutter to accumulate.

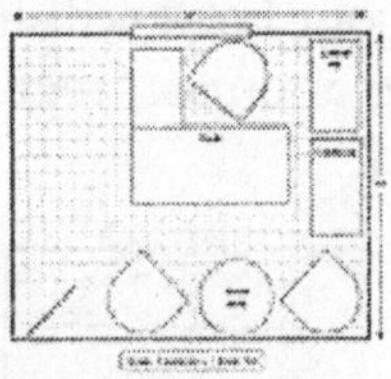

Figure 6. This layout is unbalanced with all the furniture on one side of the room, leaving little space for a comfortable traffic pattern.

In Figure 7, the same space is configured differently, with the desk facing the corner of the office and the other furniture spaced fairly evenly about the room.

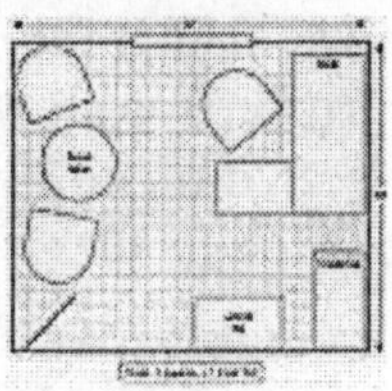

Figure 7. See if you can find the five problems present in this office layout.

Although this layout is slightly better than in Figures 5 and 6, there are still flaws to be noted. See if you can identify the problems with this layout for yourself before looking at the list following the figure. Here are the problems with this office organisation:

— The door swings and hits one of the guest chairs.

— The lateral file and the credenza being at right angles to each other creates an odd "dead space" between them when the furniture is not being used.

— The lateral file being positioned so close to the front of the credenza makes it difficult to open the credenza doors.

— The position of the desk in relation to the lateral file and credenza forces you to walk in an awkward half-circle pattern to access either piece of furniture.

— The window at your back will likely cause a sun glare on your computer monitor, regardless of where on the desk it is located.

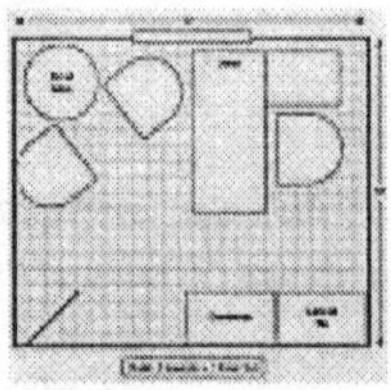

Figure 8. This layout is the most effective, using the same furnishings as in the other figures

Figure 8 illustrates how, using the same amount of floor space and the same furniture as shown in earlier examples, you can create an effective office layout. The reasons this plan works are as follows:

— The desk is far enough away from the door to offer an unobstructed view of whoever comes into the office.

— The desk is situated so you not only have a perfect view of the door, but you also have an easy view outdoors, which adds to your enjoyment of the space.

— The lateral file and credenza are grouped side by side on the opposite wall, offering easy, direct access to both pieces. This configuration offers not only a consolidated footprint, but also a large flat work surface for storing Zone Two items or projects.

— The small table and guest chairs are placed so they are out of the way, but still facilitate conversation. It is easy for guests to interact with the person behind the desk.

— The furniture is arranged so there is space to walk comfortably between all the pieces without bumping your hips or knees. The room feels larger with this much free space between pieces.

— There is plenty of space in front of the lateral file to allow the file drawers to open easily without hitting anything.

— The front of the credenza is completely accessible, making it a good place to store Zone Two items.

— The office chair has plenty of room to be pushed back and swivel around behind the desk and it is just a few steps to either the lateral file or the credenza.

— The desk is positioned so even though it is in front of the window, the sun will never be over your shoulder, placing a glare on the screen.

When placing peripherals such as printers, fax machines, scanners and such, be aware of your health and safety. Be sure that the furniture holding the equipment is sturdy enough to support its weight, and is positioned to avoid excessive bending, twisting, and leaning backward while seated.

The previous illustrations have shown you what a big difference furniture placement can make in a room. You can see how an office can feel cramped, small, and uncomfortable based completely on the furniture layout. On the other hand, you've also learned how that same office can feel spacious and comfortable simply by arranging the furnishings to create balance and logical traffic patterns.

— Consider the impact of colour and lighting on your working style

— Choose a colour scheme that fits your style and your profession

Choosing the Right Colours For Your Office

If you work for yourself or you work for a company that encourages and permits you to personalise your office, good for you! You'll have more freedom as you go through this process, and ultimately, you'll be able to create a space you love because of the latitude you're given regarding your office décor.

Colour and lighting can have a direct affect on how you feel, your mental state, and your productivity. A colour you might use in your kitchen, perhaps a bright yellow, might not be the best colour for your office because it could be too visually stimulating, making it difficult to focus and concentrate.

When choosing paint colours and décor, begin by imagining how you want your office to feel when you enter it. You also need to consider what you do for a living when choosing a colour scheme.

Importance of Colour and Lighting

If you are an artist or you work in a creative field such as graphic design or fashion design, you might want a space that is bright, cheerful, and inspires your creativity. If you have a lot of flexibility in creating your office décor, you could also opt to go with a specific décor theme, such as Asian, French Country, or even something super modern, combining stark black, gray, and white with brightly coloured accents and white metals.

On the other hand, if you work in a historically more conservative industry, such as finance, accounting, law, or medicine, where clients come into your office, you should consider using a more traditional colour and décor scheme. Neutrals such as gray, tan, white, black, and navy are a good place to begin. After you've chosen your neutral, add a complementary second colour to the scheme and a third accent colour to tie it all together.

Before you commit to a colour scheme in your head, go to a paint store and pick up a lot of paint chips. Choose more than you think you'll ever need, and don't limit yourself to a narrow range of colour choices. It's better to start with more colour options than fewer; almost any colour can look great if combined with the right complementary colours. So, even if you don't really like a colour family, resist the urge to leave it behind because you can always eliminate it later if you want to.

When choosing your colour scheme, use your imagination. When you were a kid, your imagination was strong. You could easily dream up a fortress or city when all you had was a blanket and some couch cushions. So let's rev up that imagination again for this important project. Close your eyes and imagine you're in your office and it's painted all one colour, perhaps a dark green. With your eyes still closed, tune in to how being in that dark green office makes you feel. Because colours can create very real emotions, this imagery exercise is helpful in choosing the best colours to achieve the atmosphere you want in an office setting.

Experimenting With Colour Schemes

When combining colours to make a scheme, there are a few roads to travel down, and you should consider options from each type before making a decision. Your three most basic options for an overall scheme are monochromatic, analogous, and complementary. A monochromatic scheme means you are using a single colour, but working with various values (lightness or darkness) of that same colour to create contrast and interest.

A monochromatic colour scheme is very easy for the eye to look at, and offers a sophisticated, calming, elegant look. For example, a monochromatic scheme in the brown family would have the walls painted a medium taupe, a lighter taupe on the trim with accents of rich, dark taupe in the art and accessories. A monochromatic scheme in the blue family might use pale blue walls, art, and accessories with dark blue ceiling and trim.

In contrast, the analogous scheme combines three colours that are adjacent to each other on the colour wheel, such as blue, blue-green, and green. An analogous scheme is soothing to the eye like a monochromatic scheme; however, it is a bit more interesting than a monochromatic scheme because it offers more contrast and variety. One colour is used as the dominant colour, and the others are used in fairly even amounts to enhance and support the dominant colour. An example of an analogous scheme would be three white walls with a blue accent wall, combined with art and accessories in colours of blue-green and green.

Avoid combining cool colours (blues, greens, purples) with warm colours (yellows, reds, oranges) in an analogous scheme. Your room will feel more comfortable and cohesive if you stick with either all warm or all cool colours when using this scheme.

The third basic colour scheme is called complementary, which means combining colours that are opposite each other on the colour wheel, such as orange and blue or green and red. A complementary scheme creates a high contrast level in the space and causes visual tension by combining cool and warm colours in the same scheme. In this type of scheme, one colour should be strongly dominant, with the secondary colours being used mainly as accent colours.

Examine your paint chips in the existing room light when the sun is up and when it is down. Light changes colour, so your office will look different depending on the time of day and the light source present. No matter what colour scheme you choose, monochromatic, analogous, or complementary, it has to be one you feel comfortable and at ease using.

Highlighting with Tints

When using any colour scheme, you can substitute a tint of one of your colours for white if you choose to. A tint is made by adding just a few drops of colour to bright white to create an extremely pale colour, which acts as a white without being quite so stark. You can also use a subtle pastel colour in combination with bright white for a very clean, open look.

— Determine whether you can replace the flooring in your office, or can simply cover up existing flooring
— Consider concrete, hardwood, carpeting, or "green" flooring options for your office
— Choose window treatments that provide the best lighting, privacy, and appearance

Choosing Floor and Window Treatments

The flooring in your office will help shape the overall look and feel of the space. A concrete or tiled floor looks and feels industrial, carpet absorbs sound and gives a lush executive look, and wood or laminate flooring is sleek and contemporary. More and more companies are using "green" flooring, which means they are made from natural, but rapidly renewable resources such as cork, bamboo, sisal, and other natural grasses. These materials are all examples of green flooring products that are widely available for commercial use.

If you work in a cubicle, you won't have to worry about window treatments. However, if you have your own office, you might have a window. If you're lucky; your window brings in a lot of natural light and gives you a nice view outdoors. One thing to remember about windows is that they are only wonderful when you can control the light coming in. This means using some kind of treatment over the window to either partially or completely block or direct the sunlight. Window treatments also offer privacy, which is important to many people.

Considering Your Flooring Options

Concrete flooring can be stained and etched to make it very attractive and it might have the industrial, edgy look you want in your business. However, it's hard on your feet and legs if you do a good amount of standing in your work, so add soft cushiony area rugs in the spots where you sit and stand. The addition of rugs or soft mats will increase comfort as well as add texture to an industrial space. Here are some things to consider about popular flooring choices:

— Wall-to-wall carpet is comfortable and most commercial grades are durable and attractive. Choose a carpet with a pile that is short, tight, and level or tightly looped for the greatest durability, especially in high traffic areas.

— Hardwood floors are beautiful, but like most types of flooring they require maintenance to look their best over a long lifetime. Use area rugs or floor runners to add warmth to the room and protect high-traffic areas.

Carpet tiles are also a great way to have the look of custom-made commercial rugs without the expense. You can use a single colour for a clean, monolithic look or vary the colours and textures of the squares to create an interesting design. Carpet tiles are easy to install and repair.

— Bamboo is an increasingly popular green flooring product. Besides being attractive, bamboo is a renewable material that grows faster and is harder than many hardwoods. It's also stain-resistant, which is terrific in a business environment. When properly cared for, a quality bamboo floor can last up to 100 years.

— Natural cork is a green flooring product that has been in use for hundreds of years and is experiencing a comeback with many designers. Cork, made from a layer of water-resistant cells that grow between the inner and outer barks of the tree, is lightweight, good for insulating, and resistant to rot, fire, and termites. Cork is also impermeable to gas and liquid, and it's soft, making it a more comfortable surface for those who do a lot of standing or walking at work. Cork is more expensive than wood flooring, but its many unique benefits often outweigh the additional cost.

You might not have the latitude in your office to undertake such a project as replacing flooring. However, if you aren't satisfied with the way your floor looks or you think it conveys a negative image, consider covering it up. You can find inexpensive carpet remnants at any carpet store and have the store bind the edges for a nice finished look. Some remnants are very large, so if you find a sizable piece you could cover a large portion, if not all, of your office floor.

Adding Window Treatments

Window treatment options range dramatically in cost. The most common treatments are either shades or blinds. A blind is a window treatment with rotating slats, either horizontal or vertical, which allows you to control the light by changing the slat angle. Shades are panels of cloth or other material that move up and down to either cover or uncover the window.

Some of the most frequently used commercial window treatments are horizontal blinds, also called Venetian blinds. The upside to using a blind is that you can control the light by rotating the slats. One notable downside to using blinds, however, is that their horizontal slats tend to catch dust and require frequent cleaning to remain dust-free. This is particularly troublesome for those who are sensitive or allergic to dust and dust mites.

A beautiful fix for the dust problem with regular blinds are sheer blinds, shown in Figure 9. Sheer blinds are much like regular blinds, except that the horizontal slats are made of reinforced sheer fabric and are sandwiched between two vertical lengths of sheer fabric.

Figure 9. Sheer blinds are a wonderful hybrid product in an office setting, offering the light-softening effect and beauty of sheer curtains without the bulk.

Some other options for commercial window treatments are cellular shades, vertical blinds, and opaque roller shades. Cellular shades are one of the most popular types, not only for their looks, but also because their cellular nature provides additional insulation from heat and cold. They are constructed using two layers of fabric with an open cell of fabric between that traps air and acts as an insulating layer.

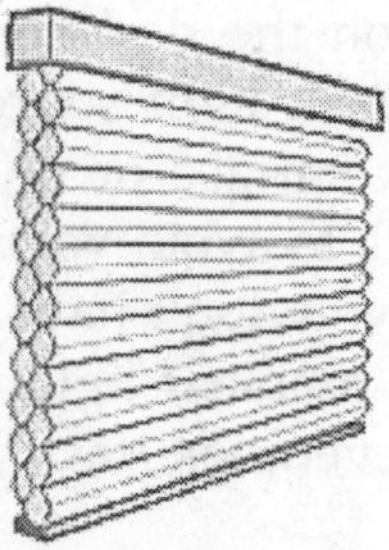

Figure 10. This side view of a cellular shade shows the insulating cell design.

Choosing Office Lighting

The lighting in your office is an important factor when setting up your space. Many offices have overhead fluorescent lighting, while a home office is more likely to have incandescent, halogen, or both. Ideally, you should have three types of lighting in your office:

Natural lighting is the sunlight that comes in from windows or skylights. This light, although easier on the eyes than artificial light, can cause excessive heat and glare, so be sure to control it using adjustable window treatments. Sunlight is also the best light for viewing colours, so if you're an artist, opt for as much natural light as possible.

If you sit in a cubicle, you won't have a window, so you'll have to work exclusively with artificial lighting. Halogen lighting is bright and as close to natural sunlight as you can get.

— Ambient lighting is the light that comes from overhead lighting fixtures. Ambient lighting in an office should be bright enough to allow you to easily see and work without falling asleep, but not so bright that it tires your eyes.

— Task lighting is focused spot-lighting used to illuminate a work surface. Task lights are fixtures that sit on the floor, on the desk, or are mounted to the wall or ceiling. Task light sources should be placed above your work surface or on the opposite side of your writing hand, to avoid your arm casting shadows on your work. If you don't have a natural light source to augment your ambient lighting or if you do a lot of work in the evenings, task lighting is especially important.

Adding Plants and Office-Appropriate Pets

Adding plants to your office or cubicle is the quickest and simplest way to increase the energy in the room and enhance the décor. In addition, plants are excellent natural air filters, which is important. The addition of healthy, beautiful plants can give you a mental boost, too, and make your room feel more inviting and comfortable. Be sure to choose plants that are suitable for the available lighting in your office and that require only as much maintenance as you will have the time and energy to give them. Low-maintenance plants such as golden pothos, schefflera, ferns, and spathiphyllum are hearty and can generally tolerate lower light levels.

If you work in a cubicle, you'll be pleased to know that you can add plants to your work area without taking up precious work space. The walls of your cubicle are called partitions, and believe it or not, you can actually mount planters on them! Visit http://www.partition-planters.com for more information about these handy planters.

If you spend a lot of time in your office and are considering keeping a pet there, be sure you have considered the responsibilities this choice will bring and that you've thoroughly researched the animal's ability to live and thrive in an office environment. Also, be sure that your building and/or management allows such pets. An office pet requires much more maintenance than an office plant and if you travel frequently or are otherwise out of the office much of the time, it's not a good idea to house an animal there alone.

Ask a veterinarian about the animal's physical and social needs. Most animals need daily watering, feeding, and exercise, and many are social creatures that require the company of other living creatures to thrive. Don't assume you can "fit" an animal into your office environment simply because you have room for a small cage, bowl, or other tiny habitat. You'll be more equipped to make an informed decision about whether you can commit to the maintenance an office pet requires. The last thing you want to do is buy an office pet and end up causing it harm because you were unprepared to meet its health needs.

Adding Personal Items

You'll spend about a third of your life working, so your office should be a place you enjoy. However, one problem with keeping an abundance of personal items in the office is that many people fail to limit themselves and their office becomes cluttered and unprofessional looking.

Personal items in your office can enhance the comfort of your space as well as give guests and clients conversation pieces upon which to build interaction with you and each other. When adding personal items to your office, it's important to be aware of the quantity you have and set space limits on yourself for those type of items. Otherwise, your personal things could take over and make it hard for you to work, focus, and be productive in the space.

After we organised the framework of her office and set up organisational systems so she could better run her business, we sprinkled many of her personal things around the space to add a personal touch. We installed wall shelves that acted as a gallery to show off her photos and other memorabilia that had previously been cluttering her work space. She liked her space even more than she had before because she could fully appreciate her things now that they were on display, rather than buried on a cluttered work surface.

Projecting the Right Appearance

Keeping a large amount of personal items and memorabilia in your office can also project a less than professional image, depending on your industry. For example, those in the financial, medical, legal, accounting, or tax industry should more carefully choose the personal items they have in their offices. These are historically more conservative fields, and clients might be put off by an overabundance of personal things in the office.

Bear in mind that your work surfaces are for working and storing Zone One materials. If you use these important work spaces for personal items, you are robbing yourself of prime real estate.

Rather than randomly placing personal items on any flat surface, choose spots that are out of the way but still allow you to enjoy your items. Place plants on windowsills or on a table next to a window; place framed photos on the top of your desk's hutch; use the top of your credenza or lateral filing cabinet to hold sculptures or trophies; and hang diplomas, certificates, and awards in Zone Two wall space.

Conversely, those working in fields such as art, music, theatre, retail, and design have a bit more latitude when it comes to what clients and superiors expect in the display of personal items at work. These fields are more creative and free-thinking, and clients often expect to see brighter colours, more whimsical or humorous art, and a larger quantity of fun and personal items in the space.

Create Your Own Art Gallery

You can create an attractive "gallery" to display personal items in the office if they are too important to discard. Just like an art gallery is a collection of art gathered in a single place, your office gallery will be your own collection of important personal items, grouped together on display.

For example, hang a few attractive shelves and designate them as your personal gallery where you can display photos, awards, sculpture, or memorabilia. Because the shelf space is self-limiting and only offers so much display space, you will be forced to carefully evaluate what you choose to keep in that space, which will automatically help you avoid clutter.

Finding and Maintaining Right Balance

Establish rules regarding how many personal items you will permit to live on your desktop. Any personal items living in Zone One are taking space away from other things that could be living there instead. Make sure personal things live above or to the sides of the desktop and out of the way of your work. Personal items should be fit into your space after your functional foundation is laid. Art, photos, memorabilia, and such are like the sprinkles on a cupcake-first you frost the cupcake and then you add the sprinkles, and not the other way around.

Periodically ask a friend or co-worker to look at your space to check for personal clutter. It's good to get an objective viewpoint because after a while your brain stops seeing the clutter. Someone else's objective eyes will see what yours have stopped seeing long ago.

To create visual interest and keep your décor fresh, rotate various personal items into and out of your space from time to time. Good points for switching items around are the beginning of each quarter, or with each new season. Changing old items out for new ones is a good way to keep your clutter level low, while still enjoying all your things. Keeping the décor fresh will also help maintain the energy level of your office and ignite your creativity all at the same time.

Displaying personal items in your office is a wonderful way to help maintain that important balance between life and work. A comfortable, balanced office shows signs of the hobbies, travel, relationships, or interests of the person within. Remember, the goal is to create an organised space where you can enjoy being, feel successful, and be productive.

Habit of Decluttering

Schedule a small chunk of time to regularly review the paper that is lurking in your office and handle it appropriately-file it, act on it, schedule action for it, discard it, or delegate it. Regularly reviewing and processing the paper in your office means you will never again have to go to the effort of sifting through mountainous heaps of paper that are months and sometimes years old.

Taking a small amount of time to declutter paper buildup on a consistent basis is more effective than taking an entire day each quarter to deal with it. Doing a little bit every day takes only a few minutes, whereas if you put it off for later, you saddle yourself with a long and arduous task you'll probably only be able to do on a weekend, when you'd rather be relaxing at home.

New habits are often hard to get accustomed to, even if they are positive and effective, so give yourself some time to adjust. Don't assume that the new habit isn't working simply because you're finding it difficult to remember to do it or you find yourself reverting to old habits. During that transitional period, you might backslide, which is normal. Don't be discouraged. Just do your best to stay focused on the positive result your new habit will make in your life.

Being organised includes using your time wisely, so regularly schedule small slots of time to maintain your organisation. Begin by doing weekly paper review and cleaning off your desk each Friday before leaving for the weekend. After you discover the productivity and confidence-boosting benefits of coming in to a clean, organised desk on Monday morning, you are likely to start cleaning off your desk every day before leaving work.

13

Winner Front Office

Winner Front Office (FO) is a professional Hotel Management System. It is a powerfull and robust system that offers advanced functionality to manage your hotel business. Winner FO is designed to meet the varied requirements of any size hotel or hotel chain and provides the tools to help you run your operation at a greater level of productivity and profitability than ever before.

Winner FO includes features such as reservations, front desk, cashier, housekeeping, night audit, system set up and over 200 standard reports. With an advanced touchscreen interface, winner FO puts all the information you need literally at your fingertips, from reservation information to rates, availability and much more. Moreover, winner FO can be extended with any type of interface, or even with fully integrated modules for Conference and Banqueting or Point of Sales as well as Stock Control management.

Profesional Solution

Winner FO is a complete Front-and Backoffice solution for Hotels, Resorts and hotel chains. It is a state-of-the-art Property Management System utilising Microsoft Windows, touch-screen technology and integration with

Microsoft Office. The applications are configurable to your specific requirements making it easy to use and to obtain fast, accurate, up-to-the minute information for your individual hotel or in a complex hotel environment running multiple properties.

Flexible and Efficient

Winner FO offers unique flexibility that helps you maximise operational effectiveness and bottomline performance. Whether you operate a single hotel or a hotel chain, Winner FO can be scaled to serve you business needs. The software is highly customisable, and even the screen lay-out, mandatory fields and more can be set according to your wishes. This makes Winner FO a solution you can adapt to any type and size of hotel.

Easy and Simple

Since staff turnover in the hospitality industry is often high, we've given a lot of thought on the design of winner FO. We listened to our users and we went in the field to witness how our systems were being used. As a result we came up with a system that is fast, easy to learn, intuitive and reliable.

From the beginning, winner FO has been designed with the use of a touch screen in mind. This makes winner FO one of the easiest systems of its kind, even for staff with limited experience on the system. With winner FO you can significantly improve guest service and increase guest satisfaction. Extended guest history makes it possible to recognise returning guests immediately and offer personalised service.

The Services module provides unseen functionality and gives you the ability to reserve any kind of service your customer may require. Service reservations can even have an inventory, or cost reference, and as such they will be charged automatically to the guest account after checkin.

Even at checkout, winner FO makes the most complicated situation a snap. Transferring or posting charges, splitting the invoice, creating company invoices, or simply grouping charges on a folio, it can all be done with a few touches on the screen. With winner FO checkout queues will become a thing of the past.

Reservations

Whether you are reserving for an individual guest, an event, a group, tour or travel agent, winner FO uses one single reservation form. This makes it extremely easy for your staff to learn the reservations process. Using the customer database, returning guests information is linked to the reservation in a matter of seconds.

Information such as availability, rates and meal plans can be accessed with one single touch. Searching the correct rate happens automatically based on the reservation details. Using winner FO you can easily handle individual, shares, group or option reservations, as well as manage waitlists and denials. Confirmation letters or rooming lists for groups can be printed at any time. Reservations are confirmed using different guarantee types like 6PM, guaranteed and deposit. The use of market codes during the reservation process can generate a detailed market segmentation of revenue figures.

Winner FO offers unseen flexibility when it comes to guest accounting. For example, a reservation can have an unlimited number of folios making any combination of bills and invoices possible. Our unique tools such as 'charge routing' and 'charge referencing' make it possible to pre-define the number of invoices and their content. As a result, upon checkout the guest will automatically get the invoices as requested, no additional manipulations are required.

An extensive library of reports lets you manage the reservations department in a very efficient manner. You can analyse historical data or look ahead and anticipate using winner FO's detailed and clear forecast reports.

Reception

With winner FO checking in guests is a single step action. One click will perform the check-in, room key will be made, the telephone extension will be opened, and a welcome message displayed on the television. An intuitive and interactive room rack makes it very simple to manage in-house rooms.

From this Rack screen you can handle all actions required for posting, services management, and even room status changes. Cashiering is very straightforward and is integrated in the reception screen. One click brings up the posting screen and the posting menu is one of the easiest in its kind.

From the Checkout screen, folios and invoices can be requested or consulted at any time during the guests' stay. In order to facilitate a flexible checkout process, folio handling has been made very easy. Folios can be readily added or removed; charges can be transferred or corrected with a minimum of effort (subject to user permissions).

Financial Accuracy

Winner FO offers full invoicing functionality with unseen capabilities. Postings and cashiering are done using a very simple and easy 'POS' like screen; no need for your staff to learn and remember posting codes or numbers. With a touch of a button you can post a charge, and winner FO will make sure revenues are recorded and invoices tracked. Winner FO has a detailed, fully configurable Trial balance, and can trace up to 14 accounting periods. Winner FO also offers a range of interfaces to Back Office Accounting systems. No need to pay your accountant for re-keying invoices into the accounting system, it can all be done seamlessly and a lot faster.

Housekeeping

Winner FO offers a housekeeping module that provides easy room status management. The housekeeping department has real-time access to the status of each room, and with an interface to the PABX the room can be set to clean via the telephone in the room. With labour forecasting, your housekeeper has an accurate view on the workload to be expected for the coming days, and a linen scheme provides details on which rooms need fresh linen.

Tours and Groups

Winner FO offers very easy tours & group handling. Tour groups usually arrive all at the same time and with winner FO, you can prepare the group check-in beforehand. Upon arrival, one click will check in the complete tour group. Guests in event groups, wedding parties or convention groups usually arrive one by one. Even this type of group is very easy to handle in winner FO.

Rooms can be picked up one by one, or checked-in individually, and can arrive on different times and even different dates. winner FO also offers fast tools for group checkout. Rooms with extra charges within a group can be identified immediately making it easy for checkout. Invoices can be generated in batch for the whole group, and automatic checkout of a group is done with one click.

'One Step' Day End

Winner FO lets you run your day end with one single click. The process is fully automated, posts all charges to the guest folios, and generates a series of reports predefined according to your needs and requirements.

Accounts Receivable

Winner FO offers an integrated accounts receivable module that lets you follow-up on unpaid invoices. You can create your own reminder letters, and these can automatically be printed in batch. Ageing calculation, credit limits and payment period limits give you full control of the hotel's receivables.

Customer Management. winner FO automatically collects customer information and builds it into a database with invaluable marketing information. The customer database is a centralised information store that keeps all information relating to your guests, companies, agents and more. Reservations, charges, room nights and much more, it can all be stored along with the customer record.

Throughout the system, this information can be consulted anywhere at any time, and you always have an accurate and up to date view of your customer. The data stored in the customer database is also used for marketing and sales purposes. Queries can be created to select customers based on the historical or production criteria. These queries are then applied to create mailing lists or to print labels and envelopes.

Internet Enabled

Winner FO can be extended to be more than just a property management system by linking it to the Fastbooking web-reservations system. This provides an end to end solution for your ecommerce activities. Your customers can confirm reservations directly from the hotel's web-site.

True Integration

All Winner products share the same integrated database resulting in a single solution for Hotel, Sales & Catering, Stock Control and even Point of Sale. Yes, even our Point of Sale product can form an integrated part of the winner FO platform which makes us unique in the industry. Our true integration means a single platform to automate all hotel departments and as a result, significantly reduce the required investment in hardware, implementation and training.

With an integrated database, hotels will no longer have to make use of interfaces to share data between these systems. Instead, users will share the same inventory, customer and account information, rate availability and controls throughout the business.

No Limits

Winner FO is an open system and offers interface possibilities to various systems such as telephone centrals, pay-tv systems, minibar and more. This close integration means significant cost savings, reduces workload and ensures that revenues are posted accurately to the guest account.

Committed

As a leading provider of hotel and restaurant technology, we offer you more than 15 years of experience in this area. Our industry expertise makes it possible to deliver solutions that work for you. You can count on us to stand behind our products and we provide support that excels on all levels. We guarantee you that by choosing winner you will have a top-notch solution today and in the future. Winner will help you remain competitive by providing a system that keeps pace with today's and tomorrows technological evolution.

Bibliography

Baker, S. Bradley, P. Huyton, J., *Principles of hotel front office operations*, Cassell: UK, PB, ISBN 0304327298, £17, 1994.

Dix, C. and Baird, C., *Front Office Operations*, Longman: UK, PB, ISBN 0582319315 £15.99, 1998.

Gray, William S., *Hotel & Motel Management and Operations*, 4th ed. Upper Saddle River, NY: Prentice-Hall, 2003.

Henkin, Shepard, *Opportunities in Hotel and Motel Management Careers.* Chicago, Ill. : VGM Career Books, 2001.

Kasavana, Michael L., *Managing Front Office Operations.* Lansing, Mich.: Educational Institute of the American Hotel & Motel Lodging Association, 2001.

Kavanaugh, Raphael R., *Supervision in the Hospitality Industry.* East Lansing, Mich. : Educational Institute of the American Hotel & Lodging Association, 2001.

Hall, C.M. and Macarthur, S. (eds), *Integrated Heritage Management'*, Stationery Office:UK, PB, ISBN 0112905714, 1998.

INDEX